ROXANE
GAY
BOOKS

RACEBOOK

Also by Tochi Onyebuchi

Harmattan Season
Goliath
(S)kinfolk
Rebel Sisters
Riot Baby
War Girls
Crown of Thunder
Beasts Made of Night

RACEBOOK

A Personal History of the Internet

TOCHI ONYEBUCHI

ROXANE
GAY
BOOKS
New York

Copyright © 2025 by Tochi Onyebuchi

All rights reserved. No part of this book may be reproduced in any form or by any electronic or mechanical means, including information storage and retrieval systems, without permission in writing from the publisher, except by a reviewer, who may quote brief passages in a review. Scanning, uploading, and electronic distribution of this book or the facilitation of such without the permission of the publisher is prohibited. Please purchase only authorized electronic editions, and do not participate in or encourage electronic piracy of copyrighted materials. Your support of the author's rights is appreciated. Any member of educational institutions wishing to photocopy part or all of the work for classroom use, or anthology, should send inquiries to Grove Atlantic, 154 West 14th Street, New York, NY 10011 or permissions@groveatlantic.com.

Any use of this publication to train generative artificial intelligence ("AI") technologies is expressly prohibited. The author and publisher reserve all rights to license uses of this work for generative AI training and development of machine learning language models.

FIRST EDITION

Printed in the United States of America

First Grove Atlantic hardcover edition: October 2025

Library of Congress Cataloging-in-Publication data is available for this title.

ISBN 978-0-8021-6625-8
eISBN 978-0-8021-6626-5

Roxane Gay Books
an imprint of Grove Atlantic
154 West 14th Street
New York, NY 10011

Distributed by Publishers Group West

groveatlantic.com

25 26 27 28   10 9 8 7 6 5 4 3 2 1

To Sarah K.
for the memes and for the memories

CONTENTS

Web 3.0: Content

Is This a Race Book?   3

Web 2.0: Contention

Prometheus, Patched: The Folly of the Metaverse   29

I Have a Rendezvous with Death   46

Pretty Woman   63

Stand Alone Complex; or, The Great American Internet Novel   77

White Bears in Sugar Land   94

I Have No Mouth and I Must Scream: The Duty of the Black Writer During Times of American Unrest   114

Select Difficulty   132

Deus in Machina   150

You'll Find Me in Heaven Before You Find Me
in a *Call of Duty* Lobby   162

Web 1.0: Contentment

Complicated German Words Regarding Memory   185

Acknowledgments   229

References   231

RACEBOOK

Web 3.0: Content

Is This a Race Book?

It's been several years, maybe the better part of a decade now, but I still feel a frisson of disbelief limning the delight that thrills me every time I see a Black cosplayer. Debate spanning generations has established Piccolo, Panthro, generally any bald character in anime with a deep voice as canonically Black; we also claim Lex Luthor and three-quarters of the cast of *Gargoyles*. But after five New York Comic Cons, a San Diego, and an Emerald City thrown in for extra seasoning, I'm still hit with an echo of that first mule kick. A city orphan stumbling through a portal into a forest full of fae adorned with Satoru Gojo's blindfold or Itachi's defaced headband or Hange's eyepatch and cape. "They're so beautiful," I whisper. And right after that, "They can't be real." It's one thing to believe you love a character in the isolation of your living room or every time you rent that DVD or video game from Blockbuster. It's another to wear that belief in a crowd, a throng filled with similarly garbed members of your congregation. And that's what it feels like now when I open TikTok and 85 percent of my For You page is anime memes and cosplay from my favorite Black creators. The authority, the fearlessness with which they claim these characters—Nobara Kugisaki, Loki, Dudley from *Street Fighter*—it's intoxicating. Joyful. The internet gave us this, gave us the power to claim these things en masse, in public, in the name of our Lord and Savior Mikasa Ackerman.

Cosplay is synecdoche for the internet. The agglomeration of your fascinations, your preoccupations worn on your literal sleeve, rendering porous the boundaries between you and that fascination/preoccupation to the extent that you may have to be told that keeping up with the Kardashians is not a personality; the grouping-together of the like-loving; the lived consequences of our new Frankenstein's monster of an identity whenever we encounter or interface with others, sweatily tactile. Whatever the internet is, it feels like it is this. The coin's shadowed side: this two-way meshing of the self and the fascination, the abrasion such that any outsider critique of the thing we love is automatically so vicious that it becomes a slight against our character. Not liking *The White Lotus* incites a moral judgment; preferring a Scorsese film—any Scorsese film—to Marvel's cinematic oeuvre becomes a mark of ecclesiastical superiority. Culture as religion, minus the sublimity and the palliative of knowing an omnibenevolent deity is working tirelessly and circuitously for your material and spiritual benefit but with all the sectarian violence. Take out all the beauty but leave the Inquisition. And every religion needs its prophets, the ones who knew that Essential Truth™ first and who are thus empowered to lead the rest of us neophytes to the Promised Land of Good Taste.

Hipsterism predates the internet, but the internet has turned a slingshot into a shoulder cannon.

There is another side to this. Call it the Anxiety of Influence.

Most of the reasons I'm as online as I am have to do with me. But some of them have to do with the people who pay me. And I suspect it's this way for a not-insignificant number of people who create things for public consumption. Publishers try to get you to post TikToks; record labels and gallery owners and streamers and whatever push you to post on Instagram; newspapers and magazines nudge you onto X (Alas, poor Twitter! I knew him, Horatio), where you can cultivate both sources and influence. And all of it so you can "grow your audience," which is shorthand for sending your flock to that glowing saffron Add to Cart button.

The consumer worries, in a dark instant, if loving a thing and not telling the world about it is keeping food out of a person's mouth. Word of mouth as business model. Word of mouth as contractual obligation. I'm sure there's a name for the economic concept of shifting this labor of promotion from factory to factory worker and another still for shifting that labor of promotion from factory to consumer. But microecon was my worst grade in college.

For a very loud time, I raved online about the things I loved in the hopes that enough people would love them too. There is, of course, a rush of satisfaction in having one's artistic diet validated by others, but, more urgently and more simply, I wanted the people making those things I loved to continue to be able to make them. "Watch this show because it's good" turns into "Watch this show because if it gets high enough ratings, the CEO of Warner Bros. Discovery won't cancel it." The hypervisibility of market forces infects cultural consumption with the flavor of the existential. The livelihoods of the musician, the video game studio, the novelist, the comic book penciller are constantly at stake. To stem the existential malaise of this permacrisis, we try to love the things they make as loudly as possible. The thing about talking online is that people talk back, and for some, that thrills. We did, after all, flock to the early internet to make fan pages for the anime and musicians we loved. But I find I rather enjoy going to the movies alone. I find I rather like being surprised by a thing. I find I rather like letting that thing do its quiet, alchemical work on my insides without the footnotes of other people's opinions. Let the result of the thing, of having seen or heard or played the thing, show in my hands. In my eyes. In the things I write. In the things I make.

When did this happen? Growing from the adolescent who loves loudly into the curmudgeon who prefers playing *God of War Ragnarök* off-stream, who keeps 98 percent of his gushing over *Industry* offline. When did I retreat? When did I disavow my stentorian duties as a public patron of the arts? I suspect it has to do with the realization that I had become data. But I think it started earlier. At some point during my time on the internet, the demographic markers I thought I'd shed whenever I logged on had latched back on to me. Gone was the faceless, skinless enjoyer of things, the amorphous yet singular netizen whose only color was that of the internet's neon signs glowing on me.

Suddenly, it seemed tremendously important that I was Black.

It did at times feel as though Trayvon Martin was on trial, which is perhaps why so many people called it—and still call it—the Trayvon verdict. Though the dictionary definition of the word "verdict" is decidedly neutral, an intimation of guilt hangs over the word. On July 13, 2013, George Zimmerman was acquitted of second-degree murder in the shooting death of Trayvon Martin, but an American verdict needs a guilty party, and Martin, like so many Black boys before and after him, presumed guilty from cradle to grave, could no longer defend himself. So, taking to the streets, taking to Twitter, taking to Facebook, we defended him.

The "we" in this case was different from any "we" I'd ever known before. I'd been among the "we" of law students, of overeducated millennials who were shot out of college and into the Great Recession, the "we" of the Toonami Generation, the "we" of Obama voters, Pats fans, *Fast & Furious* fanatics, Francophiles, people who listen to Metallica, people who listen to Metallica and Wu-Tang, people who within their first week of high school watched planes crash into the Twin Towers; but all of a sudden, that no longer mattered. The tidal wave of social upheaval had dashed away every identitarian edifice I'd spent a life constructing. The most important thing now, the most salient, was that I was the same color as that slain boy from Miami Gardens who had breathed his last bloodied breath under a night sky in Sanford, Florida, on his way back to his father's to watch an NBA All-Star game.

In law school, on Facebook, I was nothing if I was not Black. Not even my identity as a writer escaped the apocalypse of this societal climate event. Tochi was no longer a writer; he was a Black writer. A writer of Black Things™. The piece of writing that, to this day, has garnered me the most attention—the most acclaim, the most accolades, the most breathless commendation—was an angry novella birthed during those incendiary years about a boy who goes to jail and his sister who breaks the world in revenge.

From 2013 through 2015, many publications wrote about online radicalization. Indeed, on both sides of the color line, I've heard people point to Zimmerman's acquittal in the shooting death of Trayvon Martin as the catalyst for their epiphanic event, the lightning strike on their Road to Damascus. Organizations run by Black activists saw a swelling of their ranks. White supremacist organizations, militias, and reading groups saw an augmentation of theirs. It was as though sleeper cells had been activated. It's like Neo at the end of *The Matrix*, who doesn't learn how to fly so much as realize he's been capable of it all along. In *The New York Times* and the *London Review of Books*, you could read about young Muslim men and women, bristling under an increasingly oppressive surveillance regime in the United Kingdom, who were now fleeing to join ISIS. In *WIRED*, you could read, however belatedly, about disillusioned white people (often men), swirling in the unfulfilled promise of the American Economic Dream, being borne by online river currents to some of the darkest corners of YouTube. We learned about places like 4chan and, eventually, 8chan. We learned about those bituminous segments of Reddit, those pockets of rhetorical postapocalypse where the agora looks less like the town square of Thessaloniki and more like something out of *Mad Max: Fury Road*. And eventually we would see articulated in print this thing that was happening to millions of Black people across the United States who were suddenly having to do battle in Facebook comment threads with people they'd known all their lives, people they'd assumed would know which side was right and which side was wrong, people they realized had never truly known them at all.

That's what it was for me. A Great Unveiling. White classmates from elementary school, Asian classmates from high school, the Italian American father who'd shoveled snow from my mother's driveway during those winters when her children were off at school and she lacked able bodies. All of these and too many more revealed to me that vast gulf of unknowing that had separated us without my even noticing. And it all happened online. The moment had found us squarely in the midst of Web 2.0, a space of comment threads and hypercharged interaction, of dynamic social media, the animated gifs and embedded MP2s, the fan pages and whatever wholesomeness Yahoo! message boards once possessed long a thing of the past. In Web 2.0, we're not yet firmly gripped by cryptotech, large language models, and the widescale online weaponization of misinformation, but those things have passed through our opened front door and are hanging their coats up on the rack, folding their umbrellas, shaking off the rain, and not bothering to wipe their shoes on the doormat. What was once playground is now battlefield.

Thinking about the Arab Spring and about how many of the marches to celebrate the life of Michael Brown were organized online, I wonder how different a Web 2.0 version of the April and May of 1992 might have looked to us, non-Angelenos and Angelenos alike. When it was Web 1.0, the internet had the feel of something separate, a place we went to feel good about things, to learn. It hadn't yet permeated the American household. That time of America Online discs and

56k modems, when only your wealthy friends could afford DSL or cable connections, when you couldn't be online and on the phone at the same time. How differently might Los Angeles have organized itself—how differently might the country have organized itself—had we all been as online back then as we would be two decades later?

The internet before Trayvon's death didn't seem, to me, like the place where activism happened, where activism *could* happen. This land of LiveJournal and college selfies, of Joan Didion excerpts and *Supernatural* memes living side by side on Tumblr, this place you could go to and read up on the peregrine falcon, suddenly it had been turned into sword and shield in the battle for the Republic. It was thrilling. The internet was no longer just personally useful. It had transmogrified into a tool for social engineering. I belonged to a new "we," and I could be in service to them, to us. I could write and write and write. And, everywhere, I wrote. I wrote essays on law and Blackness for an online magazine a law school classmate had started. I wrote a short story about a group of Black and brown brick stackers left behind in a climate-ravaged New Haven. I wrote Facebook post after Facebook post, and suddenly the comments began to spiral into the dozens, and in these comment threads I wrote even more, and suddenly, when I looked up, this space had been turned into a town square of its own. Or rather, a pulpit. People came to hear what I was saying, what I was sharing, my lamentation, my rage, my fear, my hope. So much of me, sprayed online, and it felt like a duty, giving people something articulate to bear witness to. Something to agree with. Screeds, sermons—it didn't matter as long as it was posted.

I'd joined a new "we," and in the process, my friends became my Followers.

I can feel the gray in my beard more acutely whenever I wax lyrical about a time on the internet when a large follower count wasn't the point. Before "clout" was currency. Back when an audience was definitionally small and Sharing felt less like broadcasting a thing to as many people as possible and more like what we would ask children to do in daycare. There's an enticing counterfactual threaded through all of this. If the Alliance of Motion Picture and Television Producers had not tried in 2007 to fence screenwriters out of royalties in streaming, we might not have witnessed Vesuvius erupt its glut of reality television onto our Pompeii. Sure, the Bronco chase and MTV's *The Real World* had already begun twisting up popular ideas around celebrity; we were already being inculcated with the idea of fame with no remarkable skill or accomplishment attached, of being famous simply because one was (rich and) famous. But with the dearth of scripted television, the lane was wide open for *Here Comes Honey Boo Boo*, *Jersey Shore*, *The Celebrity Apprentice*, *Hell's Kitchen*, *I Love New York*, and, with them, the idea that any American's face not only *could* grace a TV screen, but perhaps should. Had not celebrity undergone this democratization, we might not have made it to the internet of today, with its follower counts and retweets, its Substacks and its TikToks. Is the gladiatorial roar we expectorate when someone is voted off the island any different in tone or timbre or velocity from the clamor we create when we watch someone become Twitter's Main Character?

It's not that we were unaware of the *cinéma factice* at work in reality television, but at a certain point, the scripted unscriptedness loses novelty, so the quest for vitality boomerangs back to authenticity. *True* authenticity, whatever that means. A rawness of human experience, the sheen of celebrity exchanged for the more enticingly natural iridescence of gasoline in a puddle of rainwater. That place where cringe sharpens into an actual number on the pain scale. Which brings us back to pain and the mid- to late 2010s.

I truly don't think that those gatekeepers of American culture—those with the door codes to the factories that make our books and our movies and our music—actually like seeing Black Americans suffering, but I don't know if, certainly at that time, they could conceive of any other path to authenticity within the Black American experience. As though the only sonic frequency they could pick up was the dolorous register of the funeral dirge. There's also the corporate imperative at work. Those gatekeepers, positioned both within and outside of the culture, the A&R exec and the acquisitions editor alike, know all too well that there is always, always money in the banana stand.

Do we still get here in a world that never gave us a *Real Housewives* Cinematic Universe?

If the internet's mission—if it was ever given one—was to *connect* us, the new emphasis on authenticity and the self shifted the italics from *connect* to *us*. It became imperative that people knew *you* were saying the thing online, that *you* were doing the thing posted, that they log *your* face and *your* hands and *your* smile and *your* tears, that they document *your* pledges, that they praise *your* insights, that they uplift *you* and not your SpongeBob avatar. It's how Vine stars graduate to TV roles, and it's how well-meaning white Americans signal their allegiance to the project of Black liberation. Before, a bookshelf showcasing your collection of Joan Didion's and James Baldwin's oeuvres, with Robert Caro's series on Lyndon B. Johnson prominently placed next to *For Whom the Bell Tolls* and *The Sound and the Fury*, your bookshelf with Malcolm X in both biographic and autobiographic form, was only something seen by whomever you invited into your home for an aperitif. Now it's there for anyone on the other end of your Zoom meeting to admire.

Authenticity and performance wrestle inside of us whenever we open an app or browser on our phones or type a URL into Safari. Even before ring lights and makeup tutorials, before dancing trends, before the vlogs, before Xbox Live, before rage-quitting GameTubers, there was always an element of performance in our authenticity and a degree of authenticity in our online performance. It comes with the mask. Whenever you're cleverer in a LiveJournal comment than you are in person, whenever you log on to Halo 2 and shout racial epithets after you get home from football practice with your Black high school classmates, whenever there's the promise of anonymity—accepted or refused—you are performing.

Every time I got on Facebook during those intifada years from George Zimmerman's acquittal to Freddie Gray's death in the custody of the Baltimore Police Department, there was always the donning, however unconscious, of my cape and spandex. When, before, had I ever been that angry? That fervid in my fury? When had I ever been that despairing? When had my caring ever been so loud? So righteous? Looking back, I do believe the fury was genuine. But something happens whenever a person, no matter how small their audience, is made into a spokesperson. And social media, in my infinitesimal corner of the universe, had done that for me. Had done that *to* me.

Sure, liveblogging my *Mad Men* rewatch was authentically me. But publicly mourning the shooting death of Tamir Rice online somehow felt truer; at least that was the signal beamed at me from the flurry of likes and comments I received on that post. Sharing a long essay on gene editing or the raucous, criminal life of Caravaggio felt like an authentically me move. But the political stuff, the *Esquire* profile of Elizabeth Warren, the long obloquy of Ted Cruz in *The New Republic*, the examination of Barack Obama's drone policy, the exploration of the sordid, racially charged origins of conjugal visits in USian prisons, the stuff that attacked from any angle the how-did-we-get-to-this-moment of it all—that seemed more like the Me that I had become. "You either die an inoffensive Black man or live long enough to be the guy who posts Black shit," reads the caption over the image of the cigar-smoking, ice-grilling militant in his trademark black beret. So goes the meme. It's only virtue signaling if you're not possessed of virtue. Otherwise, it's being down. Authentically down. In the trenches where you're too busy trying not to die to show off. On the internet in those years, being Black and suffering online was the cultural-capital equivalent of a lottery windfall. A bounty whose deleterious effects hide themselves expertly until, at last, you turn around years later to find your life in ruins.

In the end, it always has something to do with money. We even have a tidy term for it: surveillance capitalism.

I can't entirely blame the Russians for the growth and increasing concentration of my congregation; there was always a mercantilist underpinning to what was happening to us on social media. Audiences siloed themselves. The so-called political discourse took on a more Manichaean shape and calcified. We gravitated to those we agreed with and, coincident with that imperative, those we felt we could learn from, and little did we know that the engineering nudging us along this path was done simply so that we might click on an ad and buy a sweater.

Facebook is not the only Big Bad, and it may not even have been the first. But in this collection, if villains are brought up, good money says Meta merits a mention. That all our desires, mimetic and otherwise—the things we love, the things we want to be, the community we build, the community we quest for entry into—that all of it is grist for the algorithmic mill is the event horizon of a technological innovation playing vulture capitalist with our insides. And it's able to do this because it knows so much about us, sneakily learning all this while we're out here trying to know one another a little bit better.

In 2013, the British consulting firm Cambridge Analytica hired a data scientist from the University of Cambridge, one Aleksandr Kogan, to develop a digital app that was ultimately named "This Is Your Digital Life." The original plan was to build an informed consent process that Facebook users could then agree to before completing a survey for academic use. What ended up happening was that Facebook allowed the app to collect the personal information not only of survey respondents but of their Facebook friends, acquiring data from millions of users. By 2015, reporting from *The Guardian*, *The New York Times*, *Das Magazin*, *The Intercept*, and other outlets would go on to reveal that said user data had then, in exchange for payment, made its way into the hands of Ted Cruz, Donald Trump, and, allegedly, consultants for the British political campaign group spearheading Brexit. And this is only the data misuse scandal we heard about. I remember thinking when the news broke how remarkable it was that this was the same platform that, a decade before, had served principally to host ill-framed photos of college parties.

The watershed moment when Facebook went public, when its strategy shifted from growth to monetization, is more like a waterfall. Those outside of the tech industry may have different inflection points based on their own experience of the social network, but I remember a very Cassandran curdling of the gut when the place opened up to high schoolers.

Our path from those college parties to Cambridge Analytica passes straight through the smartphone. It's difficult to overstate the role of smartphones in the monetization process. The popular shift from desktop browsing to mobile web surfing might have killed digital advertising as we knew it, had not Zuckerberg and Facebook figured out that they now stood in an informational riverbed so thick with gold it was like the sun lay at their feet. To say that the crosshatching of demographic data—zip code, age range, musical preference, marital status, gender, race, favorite vodka brand, political affiliation, education level, favorite superhero—that Facebook possessed (rather, possesses) must have had advertisers salivating would be to indulge in criminal understatement. Why atom-bomb a catchy jingle onto the airwaves when you now had a billion automated sniper rifles at your disposal? That's sometimes what it feels like when a website force-feeds me its cookies: that by clicking "Confirm My Choices," I'm removing what little armor I have and allowing myself to be shot at from dozens of different directions by retailers of all sizes demanding I purchase things I don't want but that I'm supposed to want. By joining forces with consumer credit agencies who have their own warehouses of information about the offline behavior of sentient humans, Facebook turned itself into a mammoth information-gathering operation, the scale of which dwarfs any authoritarian regime in the history of civilization. At 2.1 billion active daily users as of Q4 2023, Facebook is the world's largest country. Who knows best what's in your heart? God, your therapist, or Facebook?

However, if it wasn't clear before 2016, it was certainly made clear after the events of that fall and during the ensuing fallout that Facebook's biggest impact on human society isn't necessarily on what purchases we end up making. It's on our emotions. It seems apropos, then, that a 2012 paper in the *Proceedings of the National Academy of Sciences* refers to the act of joining Facebook and, subsequently, friend groups therein as "social contagion." A June 2014 paper in the same journal refined the idea further to "emotional contagion." The paper states:

> For people who had positive content reduced in their News Feed, a larger percentage of words in people's status updates were negative and a smaller percentage were positive. When negativity was reduced, the opposite pattern occurred. These results suggest that the emotions expressed by friends, via online social networks,

influence our own moods, constituting ... massive-scale emotional contagion via social networks.

The same paper had this to say about News Feeds:

First, because News Feed content is not "directed" toward anyone, contagion could not be just the result of some specific interaction with a happy or sad partner.

All those posts about Trayvon. All those posts about Tamir. About Alton Sterling. About Renisha McBride. About Michael Brown and Freddie Gray and Sandra Bland, about the fifteen-year-old Black girl who, on June 5, 2015, was body-slammed by a police officer named Eric Casebolt at a pool party in McKinney, Texas. All those posts about the church burnings that ravaged the South that same summer, about how the protections of the US Constitution were never meant to be extended to Black Americans, about the Supreme Court decisions, all the calls to arms, the scolding of white Americans for their ineffectiveness at stemming the tide of anti-Blackness or, worse, their apathy in the face of it, the pleas for solidarity with other non-white Americans. The outrage machine co-opting justifiable and justified outrage, amplifying it, infecting others with it. The desiccation of journalism and the pivots to video so that, increasingly, the reading public got its news from a social network's website whose raison d'être was getting us to click on things. All of it in service to a process that got its terminology from biological disease.

When it came time for Facebook to start earning money, its leaders decided the best way to go about it was to make us feel shitty.

Other social networks are powered by the same engine. It explains the toxicity of an erstwhile microblogging platform where people went to tweet about what they ate, what was going down in their corner of the Bronx, and to tell funny jokes. It explains the imperative behind Instagram's effort to turn your life into a highlight reel, coincident with the platform's dictates about authenticity. It explains what Cory Doctorow calls the "enshittification" of TikTok. I would give myself periodic shots of antidote by reading long-form nonfiction in publications like the *London Review of Books* or *Vanity Fair* or *Harper's Magazine*, and there was always the reminder that when I closed a browser window, there was the whole wide world right there outside my actual window, that internet brain wasn't terminal, or at least that it didn't have to be. Legal scholar Tim Wu calls the inevitable backlash to the mercantilization of our attention the "disenchantment effect," and perhaps the shittiness that I feel and that so many others recount feeling is simply the brain fighting back. If you didn't get a runny nose and a sore throat, the common cold would kill you. Still, the body is different after the physical rehab that follows a bout with debilitating illness. Every return to the offline world, the Facebook app closed, the browser window gone, entails a little bit of learning how to be a human being again.

Though I heard the first scratch and whine of an internet modem before I ever picked up a pen to write, I believe I was a writer before I was an internet user. Or, better put, I was a citizen of the world of words first and a car owner on the information superhighway second. But whenever I would poke my head above water and look at the career I'd managed, through no small amount of good fortune, to carve out for myself, I would see a body of work a younger self would not have recognized. Sure, some elements persisted: a strong dose of anime and manga influences, an appreciation for the utility of speculative fiction, the complications of the human heart as a narrative priority. But a narrowing had occurred. When I put those books with my name on the spine next to select others on a bookshelf, or saw them grouped together on tables in a bookstore, I realized that the central preoccupation of my career in storytelling had been race. On the heels of that epiphany came the worry that it all, in truth, boiled down to performance. That I had turned into profit the outrage-fueled posting that attended those years in the mid-2010s when the scales fell from my eyes and I emerged with a new, true understanding of where my racial identity had placed me on the chessboard of the United States. I should have felt enriched by this, as though I'd been gifted with powerful, prosthetic limbs, not having realized that, beforehand, I was living as an amputee. I should have been thrilled that I was privileged to live in a literary moment when the Powers That Be had realized the commercial potential of stories featuring non-white characters doing remarkable, horrible, complicated things. I should have felt honored. I should have felt honor. Why did I feel, instead, like I had been lessened?

The book industry endures trends as much as it perpetrates and perpetuates them. The memory of that time, when writing elegantly and eloquently on the plight of Black Americans was en vogue, is still fresh. Memoirs about how difficult it was to be a Black man in America abounded, listicles featuring "Black Authors to Read" proliferated. DEI initiatives sprang up, almost fully formed, like Athena from the very white head of Zeus. And the marriage between the preeminence of identity and the social issues at the forefront of popular consciousness had birthed a moment from which revenue could be wrung. This isn't to say that the internet is wholly responsible for making Black writers writing about Blackness popular. It isn't even to say that publishing books that tell America what's wrong with it is an entirely novel trend. It's only to say that a flattening had occurred. Nothing prevented me from writing heist novels or revenge epics set during the Tokugawa shogunate or books about the bounty hunters and space pirates I'd loved in *Outlaw Star* and *Cowboy Bebop*. Except, of course, that I was no longer that man. I was no longer that boy. To become a published author, to realize the childhood dream,

I had to know that I was little more than a constellation of commodified data points.

You either die an inoffensive Black man or live long enough to be the guy who posts Black shit.

Social media didn't make me race conscious. Around the early to mid-2010s, I was in law school learning about inequities and inequalities, race and the law. But I would be lying if I said the arguments I got into on Facebook during those years—about whether Trayvon Martin's shooting death was justified; about the wrongness of the officer-involved shooting of Tamir Rice; about why law school is the place to go in order to learn about laws, not justice—had no effect.

There is something to be said about the authority that a personal identity confers on someone when it comes to the recounting of experiences or the imaginative extrapolation of them in literature. Isn't that how we got *Go Tell It on the Mountain* and *Another Country*? Baldwin drawing from the profound well of personal experience is always a wonder worth emulating. However, the external imposition of that identity or the selection of its primary valences at the expense of everything else, that's the steamroller that turns a 4D person into a caricature. That's the cage. Imagine Baldwin unable to publish a piece of writing that didn't have as its gravitational center the glory and plight of Black Americans. Imagine Baldwin without *Giovanni's Room*.

I started this essay thinking the solution was to adopt the hermit's posture. Log off. Never mind how much it would feel like a concession, like admitting that the whole thing, the whole internet, was a net negative. For the world as for myself. And I have indeed developed a truculent resentment toward its most visible, most ubiquitous parts. But then I'm returned to the images of those Black cosplayers, and my itch for the antediluvian turns to vapor. Amid it all, amid the live-streamed massacres and the shareholder-ification of society, amid the flourishing of conspiracy theories and the flattening of identities into simple, marketable demographic badges, there they are: Satoru Gojo and Sasuke and Jotaro, and yet, all the same color as me, not either-or but both-and, and I see a way out. If I have to force-feed my own fascinations onto the page where I feel most comfortable, most powerful, if I have to cram discursions about androids and about *Neon Genesis Evangelion* and about FromSoftware video games into a book with "Race" in the title, I will do it. I have to do it.

I will write my way there. To all of me.

Is this a race book or is it not? Is it either-or? Can it be both-and?

Can I?

Web 2.0: Contention

Prometheus, Patched: The Folly of the Metaverse

It begins a little something like this:

> WEL-COME BACK TO SUPE! SUPERMARIO-MAKER! WEL-COME BACK TO SUPE! [gibberish shouting] WHAT UP! IT'S DASHIE! AND WEL-COME BACK! BACK TO WHAT?! SUPERMARIO-MAKER2! YOU KNOW! IT'S THE GAME WHERE YOU MAKE ME LEVELS, TWEET THEM TO ME [here he points to the Twitter handle that pops to life over his left shoulder], I PLAY THEM LIKE THIS [here he mimes aggressive button-mashing on a Super Nintendo controller], THEN I RAGE THE FLUUUUUUGH OUT!

Our host turns red at that last part. *Looney Tunes* smoke whistles out of his head. Then @DashieGames is a normal human male again.

There's more to his intros. There's restrained yet impulsive salsa dancing. There's an entreaty to gather snacks. There's stocktaking, what he's been up to lately. And Satan makes a cameo appearance. We don't see the Prince of Darkness, but orange flames overlay the screen, and a bass-y, syrupy, chopped-and-screwed voice descends from above with "Ayo, Dashie," followed by any number of things: a pun, some fat-shaming, or, conversely, Satan wanting to clap Dashie's cheeks. All of which gamer and internet personality Dashie rebuffs *bruyamment*.

Every intro for over a hundred of his YouTube videos begins with some variation of this. Chaotic, in need of a volume warning, and somehow vulnerable at the same time. We're not about to watch @DashieGames be good at a video game. We're about to watch him struggle. We're about to watch him rage the FLUGH out, as he puts it. We're about to hear him dive into a sea of malapropisms like "Can't be counting chickens" and "Don't wanna get traun-traun-traunched." We're about to watch a young man slowly descend into the heart of darkness, a psychedelic, effusively colored wasteland of wizards and fanged tortoises and moles that throw wrenches, growing madder in every sense of the word, losing perspective, losing his mind, until he reaches that flagpole at the end. Then he does it two more times. Toward the end of the video, the table is reset.

Our hero is left huffing and puffing and, more often than not, victorious. Like he's just survived the One-Chip Challenge. And just like those survivors, he sometimes promises he will never do that again, that the hurt is too great, but always, he returns.

It's not Schadenfreude that draws me and hundreds of thousands of viewers back time after time. We don't want him to lose. Though his *Schaden* gives us *Freude*, we want him to win. We laugh at his cockiness being punished, but we don't necessarily come in wanting a Roman holiday. Every key he attains to unlock a further section of the arena and journey deeper into the level brings us to our feet, cheering. The sounds are Pavlovian. The *dundundundadundadundadundundun* of an invincibility star, the *threep* of a jump, all markers of success, improvement, a puzzle piece fitting into place.

Watching those videos over the course of more than a year, sharing them with loved ones, I realized I'd somehow stumbled upon the Platonic ideal of community engagement. As much as Dashie seemed to suffer, he was having fun. And so were we.

I think that is what Meta is trying to re-create.

In 2021, having spent a year and change living virtually—going to school virtually, interfacing with stranded loved ones virtually, trying to figure out how to not die virtually—the idea started to percolate among a tech elite titanically unable to read the room that maybe we should go ahead and live our entire lives online. In a metaverse. A Metaverse. Physically, we would be propped up against our headboards or the wall in our studies, wearing a decreasingly bulky headset. Cognitively, emotionally, spiritually, we would be at a comedy club watching a Josh Johnson comedy set, basking in his aura of adorable awkwardness, nodding along to his sensible takes on serial killers and megachurch pastors, laughing when we were supposed to, guffawing when we weren't. Or we would be exchanging tips on childcare while crowded around a virtual park bench pushing virtual prams with virtual babies the size and shape of toxic potatoes inside of them. It was a heady time for tech, but when is it not? While, IRL, we topped a hundred million COVID cases worldwide and, that same January, watched Trump supporters turn the Capitol Building into the house from Slipknot's "Duality" music video, and while a few months later the President of Chad was killed in a coup and the global COVID death toll passed three million, and while the Israeli Air Force bombed the offices of the Associated Press and Al Jazeera in Gaza, and Derek Chauvin was sentenced to twenty-two years and six months for the murder of George Floyd, and the Sixth Assessment Report from the IPCC took on its most apocalyptic tenor—while all this was happening, Facebook changed its name to Meta. "In the metaverse," the company said, "you'll be able to do almost anything you can imagine." But presumably, hopefully, none of the above.

I don't know that the sales pitch was for us as much as it was for shareholders, money market men. Everyone I knew and a sizable chunk of people I didn't saw this for the fad it was—Bitcoin Redux or Web3 the Remix or NFTs. Another shiny ball come along for people to throw the GDP of a Micronesian nation at. There'd always be another (and there was with AI). But it didn't seem to matter that in May of 2022, so-called "stablecoins" TerraUSD and Luna would lose their one-to-one dollar pegs, Thanos-snapping away $40 billion in wealth. Fortune 500 favors the bold.

Here's Mark Zuckerberg on an earnings call in Q3 2021:

> I view this work as critical to our mission because delivering a sense of presence—like you're right there with another person—that's the holy grail of online social experiences . . . If you're in the metaverse every day, then you'll need digital clothes, digital tools, and different experiences. Our goal is to help the metaverse reach a billion people and hundreds of billions of dollars of digital commerce this decade.

He goes on to talk about the then-recent Quest 2 headset, retailing at $299; smart glasses whose brand name I've up until researching this essay never heard of; and, interestingly enough, his expectation that investment in virtual reality and augmented reality would reduce operating profit (to the tune of $10 billion) in the near term. But if I'm still wiping char off my face from a whistleblower scandal, maybe I'd pay $10 billion to get the hell out of here too. The Metaverse is an easier pitch for shareholders than it has proven to be for consumers. In 2021, I couldn't have cared less about "the successor to the mobile internet." But I was willing to risk a felony charge to get a PS5 at retail.

If I ever made it to the Metaverse, would I be following Dashie through those *Super Mario Maker 2* levels? Would I be sitting in an aisle seat while he performed his button-pressing onstage? Would the sound for his own avatar be turned off so he wouldn't have to worry about us distracting him? If I paused him to go on a bathroom break, would I be pausing him for everyone else? Very quickly the logistical concerns of the metaverse—Facebook's *Horizon Worlds* or Microsoft's "Mesh"—become more obstacle than incitement for innovation. All the things I like doing online and off, like watching *Mortal Kombat* combo tutorials and listening to clips from the ShxtsnGigs podcast and debating which is the best Christopher Nolan film with loved ones over a pasta dinner, trying to do them there would just be worse. Still, nothing we said could stop the late-2021 virtual land rush.

Here were investors literally buying non-fungible tokens that were little more than treasure maps of virtual worlds that didn't even cross over to other virtual worlds. There were dreams of what beautiful money-making things these investors would build on that land that didn't actually exist, the creator economy they would house, the coltan mines pregnant with generative human activity that they could turn to dollars. Twenty-first-century industrialists don't build railroads or universities. They apparently build countries where the Geneva Conventions don't apply.

We watched in wonder as the crypto pump-and-dump land speculation happened in real time, its subject, conceivably infinite but ever-price-pointed terrain. Maybe I'm wrong. Maybe it's not ignorance that drove this whole economic biome into an existence that has since dampened if not petered out. Maybe they knew what they were doing. Drug cartels and money launderers come to mind. A decent chunk of Manhattan real estate houses wealth rather than people. Why not bypass the meat-package altogether, the meat-package that joins pesky unions and complains to renters' rights organizations and NGOs, that petitions in housing court and is often an unreliable tenant? If you told me that the metaverse is one giant money-laundering operation, I don't know that I'd disagree with you. Maybe virtual reality as it's currently being pitched to us is just a washing machine, and all the dirt being scrubbed off that money lands on those of us who have to deal with Nintendo Wii avatars who bought NFTs that let them choose usernames that bypass the platform's prohibition on swears and slurs. Some dollars, rubles, and rials need scrubbing, so I gotta deal with some guy named

MonkeyCoon2364 who talks like someone I'd like to smash with a *Wii Sports* tennis racket.

On the surface, the metaverse may model itself on *Second Life* or some more lived-in version of *The Sims*. Or maybe there's even some anime or Neal Stephenson novel with VR or some analogue thereof as a central plot device, and maybe the maladroit men at the top of our social media ziggurats see an opportunity to craft another monument.

Mark Zuckerberg was born three years before me. It is entirely possible that, the internet having been much smaller then than it is now, we spent time on the same digital map, continents apart though we were. I don't know that I've ever heard him speak about his own experience of the internet, whether he's caught by the same longing for that simpler, smaller time. As busy and as complicated and as complex as we are now, maybe there's still that capacity for us to experience the internet as we did then, and maybe, just maybe, it can come with a dollar sign.

It can be a fool's errand, trying to empathically connect with the people out there who have more money than God, people whose lives are lived in dimensions so far removed that trying to communicate with them, to attempt mutual understanding, would be like a human talking to a dog or to an AI trapped in a black box, something that possessed demonstrable intelligence, but that could never really attend our child's christening. Still, I like to imagine.

And imagine is all I can do when trying to reason through Zuckerberg's incessant focus on the Metaverse, an idea doomed from the beginning for many reasons, not the least of which is that it is already being done better in so many other places. If he's willing to throw good money after bad, I get it. I've bet on racehorses before. But when the shareholders sound the alarm and the table he's gripped so tightly is being shaken by hands other than his own, demanding he pump the brakes, surely that should mean something. In one three-month period in 2022, Meta's Reality Labs, the division of Meta focused on VR and AR technologies, lost $2.8 billion, with a *b*. In their Q1 2023 earnings report, it would come out that Reality Labs cost Meta and its investors $13.72 billion total for 2022. The headsets are clunky and too expensive, the avatars have no legs, the virtual comedy clubs are empty. And yet Heath Ledger's Joker could not hope to burn as much money as the chairman and CEO of Meta Platforms is currently doing. Onward and upward.

So why?

I think he misses it.

I think Mark Zuckerberg is still hopping on earnings calls in 2024 and talking about the Metaverse because he misses the early internet.

Social media was, in certain lights, an attempt to recapture that feeling, the idea being that we would still somehow in the year of our Lord 2005 or 2008 or 2025 be dazed with wonder at the prospect of instant connectivity with others, and not repulsed by the notion. But social media never fully became what the early internet was. Where before nastiness might have gotten you shunned from communities, it now rewards you with followers. Where before we donned our mask for whoever might've visited our GeoCities webpage, now every meme we quote tweet is a performance before an audience of thousands. If you're (un)lucky, millions. It was too much democracy too fast.

While content monetization is ever the impellent, it is perhaps too easy an explanation for me, trying to enter Zuckerberg's thinking on his metaverse obsession. If he really, truly wanted to maximize value for his shareholders and do something he felt was ahead of the curve in that same spirit of "move fast and break things," he could have found it, and it wouldn't have been whatever the Metaverse is in his head.

In the end, I think it's his Rosebud.

Dude's human just like the rest of us, to a certain extent. Of course he might be captured by longing! Of course he might miss the way things were! Of course he's the guy who's gonna bring us there. It's that classic tension of the frailty of human longing put in the mech suit of the Übermensch.

This comparison between the early internet and the mystery at the center of *Citizen Kane* (what exactly *is* "Rosebud") grows darker when one remembers that the significance of the word—newspaper magnate Charles Foster Kane pining for the comfort of his childhood home, longing for his mother's love—isn't revealed until the very end of the movie, when the sled bearing the trade name "Rosebud" is tossed into a furnace and engulfed in flames.

The metaverse will forever be a lonely, cobwebbed place not because of its features (do the avatars have legs yet?) but because of its function.

It is not GameFAQs, it's not Yahoo! message boards. It's not a place that people run to.

Maybe the Metaverse doesn't aspire to be that place. Maybe it only wants to be the place you get to once you've finished running. No matter what it is you're running from.

The pandemic, institutional collapse, mercenary mercantilist assaults on personhood *partout*, rising rent, rising inflation, rising water levels, wildfires, institutional racism, robot dogs, mosquitoes, mask mandates, union-busting, downsizing, corporate mergers, and the butchering of Entertainment's sacred cows, maybe all of that is the collective gun to our heads forcing us into the arms of whatever the metaverse promises or believes itself to be—the place we get to when we've stopped running.

I joked with a friend in the summer of 2016 that *Pokémon* GO might just have saved the global economy. Though there was plenty of tumult in the world at the time—or perhaps *because* there was plenty of tumult in the world at the time—looking back at that summer evokes the same feel as watching that first *Fast & Furious* movie. You know how so many of those movies feel like they take place in the summer of 2001? How they, until their later iterations, always managed to feel situated in a world before 9/11? Before the surveillance state the US would become, the invasions of Afghanistan and Iraq, the Great Recession? Before *Crash*? That's how the heady, muggy summer of 2016 felt. I think we have *Pokémon GO* to thank for that.

That summer, the software company Niantic, collaborating with Nintendo, launched *Pokémon GO* and suddenly had millions of people around the world venturing from their homes and schools to parks and diners and elsewhere, meeting their future partners, creating friend groups, communing with strangers, all in the shared pursuit of elusive Eevees.

Not only did the location-based, augmented reality game gross more than $650 million USD in its first three months, it bolstered distressed businesses with increased foot traffic. It brought people to sites of historical importance all around the world. It ushered them to houses of worship.

Reddit was awash in stories of Staryu-initiated serendipity. We were a breath away from Naruto-running through Union Square. There's a photo of me at the time, taken by a belle, with a Doduo superimposed over most of my torso, and under that photo, a caption: "This is the photo they put on my membership card for the local Pokémon Go Widower Support Group."

The games officially began in July of 2016 with launches in Australia, New Zealand, and the United States. To keep the servers from buckling under the strain of outsize demand, worldwide release was staggered. By July's halfway mark, most of Europe had the game, and before month's end, so did Canada, Puerto Rico, Japan, France, and Hong Kong. August saw launches throughout Latin America and Southeast Asia, while the Balkans and much of Central Asia got the game in September, and on October 4 (my birthday), the app launched in thirty-one African countries and territories.

With an AR platform like *Pokémon* GO inevitably come moments of political surreality. A Pokégym popped up in Panmunjom, in the Korean Demilitarized Zone. Members of the Israel Defense Forces were banned from using the game because a gym might pop up on a military base. An augmented reality has ours to build off of. It can recast public monuments, changing our purpose for visiting them, but no Separation Wall ever collapsed under the weight of a Snorlax. Try as it might, the game could not turn Japan's Yasukuni Shrine into a space of social bonhomie. Instead, it became the landing site for a group of Chinese players who spoofed their GPS. A Pokégym had been placed beyond the shrine's looking glass, and nationalism had poked through. Players in Bosnia were warned that they should not hunt these monsters in minefields left over from the 1990s war.

And there is, of course, the fear that an intelligence agency or thirty might be salivating at all that location-based data being shared.

But somehow, Niantic had released the greatest stealth fitness app ever. Peloton could never.

More deeply, *Pokémon* GO understood that we are more likely to participate in an augmentation of our reality than in the wholesale construction of another. No matter how many sensory modalities are computer-mediated (or smartphone-mediated), there is still us with our bodies, our fitness apps keeping track of the day's steps. There's something of the recognizable in an augmented reality. Washington Square Park is still Washington Square Park even if that bench a few feet away is hiding a Hitmonchan. The world we recognize is the starting point. Our religions understand this too. Djinn visit us, not the other way around.

We were all doing the same thing. That's what it comes back to. A shared reality where shared meanings were injected into the spaces we inhabited, where we embarked on identifiable journeys, our aims intelligible to one another. And, at its core, it was a game. It was play. A large part of the appeal of *Pokémon* GO was that it was not a permanent state of affairs. You could put your phone down and the world would return to its former hue. Delete the app from your Android, and a church is a church again. Tracking down Seakings is enjoyable, sure, but that is, in part, because it's not the only thing I'm doing with my life. I'm not trapped in pursuit of Pokémon. That is why current efforts at VR strike me as so wrongheaded. Rather than imbue the existent with meaning, with affect, VR crafts affect, then begins to build the object. Imagine building laughter before you've built the funny cat video. Imagine building laughter.

    Pokémon GO made the companies involved in its creation so much money because we all knew what *Pokémon* was. *Pokémon* is the highest-grossing anime franchise of all time. We knew what it meant. Our kids know what it means. Ash Ketchum and company had already given us so much, including, from the beginning, the opportunity to be him, to be the very best . . . like no one ever was. Already, whether we had picked *Pokémon Red* or *Pokémon Blue* for our Game Boys, this existing thing was freighted with meaning. It could only grow from there.

The metaverse as a concept has lost its gilt, at least for companies like Disney. But Meta Connect, in September of 2023, saw Zuckerberg unveil yet another VR headset, the Meta Quest 3. Zuckerberg, during his keynote address, would have committed the gravest dereliction of duty had he not featured AI, the tech obsession du jour, but no longer was the metaverse a purely virtual phenomenon. At least, not the way he spoke about it. The hope, on that side of the San Andreas Fault, is that Meta's new smartwatch and its AR glasses will eventually replace smartphones. Most people walking by will see your old ass playing chess against an empty chair, but you'll have your old drinking buddy's face smiling back at you, all blue and holographic. Or you might attend a birthday party where most chairs are filled with living, breathing human beings and the rest with holograms. Maybe some of them are gussied-up chatbots dressed as the dearly departed. Already, I've slid into the macabre.

A friend sent me a TikTok one night of a woman at home in a floral-print top wearing a Meta Quest VR headset. She has her hands raised and, at one point, falls to her knees. Children giggle around her at points in the video or sigh sympathetically. We don't see what she sees. We don't hear what she hears. But her words are inflected with that praise-pleading that attends contact with the divine. The video is captioned "Happy mothers day 🥹." And the overlay reads: "Took my mom to Mecca In vr."

I have no sarcasm to meet the moment. No irony, no blithe dismissal or mockery. Just a silent, stunned appreciation for the thing I'm witnessing. I return to it over and over, and each time my conclusion is different. "Here's Meta's greatest ad." "I wish I could do something like this for my mother." "Maybe we all just need a little God in our machines." Until I get to the realization that's been waiting for me ever since I started this essay: This thing, whether VR or AR, is an inevitability. And so is our ability to make it mean something, to turn our tech into a vehicle for love, for connection, for significance beyond the wildest imaginings of anyone in a corporate boardroom. This thing I've spent over three thousand words disparaging is what granted that woman this religious experience. The sight is both terrifying and wondrous, blasphemous and exalting. We are watching the mountain being brought to Muhammad.

No world is more magical than the one we already inhabit. Our technology is at its most seductive, its most consequential, when it remembers and reminds us of exactly this.

Hesitant, enchanted, I whisper, "Take me there."

I Have a Rendezvous with Death

I'll never forget the day I saw my first massacre. Or rather, its fresh aftermath. It might've been in the context of the Ambazonian Crisis. It might've been Boko Haram–related. But at the beginning of the video, there's a mountain of clothed corpses, bare feet and arms smeared in red clay protruding from the tangle of stacked torsos, and around the bottom of the pile, a few corpses facing heavenward. I squint at one body in particular, crushed under the rest, with everything from the waist down out of frame. And there's a soldier in fatigues, sleeves rolled up, rifle slung over one shoulder, toeing with his boot a dislodged chunk of the corpse's skull.

When people ask, I tell them the last regular job I held before writing full-time was in "event detection." Basking in the aura of mystique, I elaborate by describing it as "knowing what's going on in the world before most other people do."

Such information is incredibly valuable, it turns out. More and more, it's how banking happens. But law enforcement pays for this information, too, as do armies, entertainment reporters, risk analysts. Everything from a terrorist attack in Barcelona to the amorous activity of the Kardashian clan, all of it mattered.

My beat had me neck-deep in political crises and vehicular catastrophes. Which meant, in essence, pressing my eyeballs up against the internet to witness, over and over again, for eight and a half hours at a time, the very worst moment in a person's life.

Often, there was no media attached to the tragedy I had to find and document. I'd have to rely on a tweet of an announcement or perhaps a foreign-language news story about a car bombing in Mogadishu or a village raid somewhere in the Sahel, a café shooting in Ouagadougou, a mass abduction in Maiduguri. Sometimes, the thing would come to me in the form of a cry for help from someone there. A virtual "oh shit" or "my God" or "somebody help" I could do nothing about except tell a person who is going to become richer by virtue of knowing about this tragedy before other people. That is its own genre of hurt, because my imagination had license to run riot. This isn't to say that watching video of vehicular manslaughter at Charlottesville is any less traumatizing than hearing or seeing people there react to it. It's only to say that the train ride home after that particular shift was quieter than usual. There's something specific and specifically horrifying, however, about having to watch a livestreamed mass shooting in a house of worship. A quirk of scheduling is the only reason I didn't have to be in that early that day.

But it was a two-day terrorist attack perpetrated by al-Shabaab on civilians in the DusitD2 hotel complex in Nairobi in 2019 that finally pushed me to develop an exit strategy for this job. I didn't see people die, mercifully. But I saw dead people. And I read tweets uploaded in real time by someone hiding in a room with no way to charge their phone, saying their location and calling for help over and over until there were no more tweets.

That first day, you're so locked in that it's all just information, and you go home afterward, having handed off the matter to the next shift, and maybe you sleep all right or maybe you try to squeeze some work in for edits on a novel coming out later that year. But then you get to the train station the next morning and, sitting on a bench and waiting to board, you see an Al Jazeera notification about the attack on your phone and you begin to sob—your own tight bundle of hurt on that wooden bench—before you pull yourself together and head back into work to pick up where the last shift left off.

Before and after that attack, there are videos of child abuse, deep-fried memes from someone whose avatar is Courage the Cowardly Dog, the mass roasting of some start-up folks who believe they've invented the bodega, a US president staring directly into a solar eclipse, car bombings, racially motivated hate crimes, hurricanes, a royal wedding, and Kendrick Lamar winning the Pulitzer Prize for Music. Among other things. So much life lived and lost, evidence of which I had to trawl for online, and it seemed like this grand technology of the internet hadn't improved us at all. By the end, it felt like it had just augmented our madness. The same year Kendrick won and Harry and Meghan married, I watched XXXTentacion die in his car after he was shot near a motorcycle dealership in Deerfield Beach, Florida.

We were supposed to have hovercars by now.

When reporting started to go wide about the plight of Facebook's and YouTube's content moderators, I felt an immediate recognition. If you're splitting hairs, their work is different from event detection, but only in color, not in sense. I felt I could understand them a bit. The dissociation; the slow-moving psychic injury, like the buildup to a stroke; seeing your sense of humor deform into an increasingly mordant shape; trauma bonding with your colleagues; not being paid nearly enough; and when raising the alarm about your deteriorating mental health, being compensated with hilariously inadequate measures like ten-minute guided meditation sessions right before your shift.

The job turned me into a Twitter "power-user." I became supremely adept at searching, at finding things out, at verifying information, at sussing out agendas, at cross-checking. I developed so many of the abilities that make for a good journalist, albeit with none of the actual footwork. I got to see so much, and perhaps more importantly, I got to see it first. And one of the greatest hallmarks of excellence in social media is to be first. Isn't that why the Contrarian is such a popular warrior class on Twitter? Pick any topic, manufacture an outré enough opinion, and be rewarded with attention, the premier currency in the online economy.

The job itself could not have possibly existed at an earlier time. I imagine, even years from now, it will seem like a job that could exist only in the future, the way Missy Elliott songs from twenty years ago still sound like they're from the future. Sure, there's the technology aspect of it. When have our fiber optic cables ever been so powerful? But walking down memory lane to arrive at a room filled with debt-ridden grads making less than $100K a year to watch beheadings and cartel executions never ceases to leave me stunned. Did we really go through that?

To properly discern its provenance, I googled the phrase "Blood makes poor mortar." The resulting page came with a prompt to "search with an AI-powered boost." Below that: "Try out a new generative AI experiment from Google," with the options "Not right now" and "Try now," the latter a much darker purple than the former.

I'd thought to use the quote from Charlton Heston's Moses in *The Ten Commandments* to start off an extended metaphor on how algorithms are the new ziggurats, the new pyramids even, and how the Pharaonic among us proclaim their magnificence, their uniqueness, in the same booming timbre they deployed in antiquity, the metaphor stretching skyward until it hit that button where I would note that just like those monuments, what we have taken in 2025 to calling AI has buried beneath it the bones of unremembered laborers, very likely underpaid, perhaps even unpaid. The metaphor would strain under its own weight.

Someone in the back, wearing an OpenAI T-shirt, would point out that those content moderators in Kenya who fed material to ChatGPT-like platforms, who reviewed text describing necrophilia and images of child abuse, were at least paid $3.74 an hour before they were summarily dismissed, their contracts terminated eight months early. I would take my chance to highlight the hellishness of their work, only to be cut off by the retort that teaching swear words to ChatGPT couldn't be all that bad. Detecting that my detractor might have more sympathy for the less-melanated, I'd mention Isabella Plunkett, a content moderator from Ireland who in the summer of 2021 testified before a parliamentary committee on just what she'd faced at her job moderating content for Facebook, through her then-employer Covalen. "And during a pandemic, no less!" I'd shout at my interlocutor, shaking my fist. And with one last glance over my shoulder as I hurried offstage, my metaphor strapped to my back, I'd tell him that the Tower of Babel was a ziggurat too.

Behind (or, rather, beneath) every algorithm is a faceless, nameless workforce, anonymized beyond the imaginings of Karl Marx, making the damned thing tick. Filching art to see the results of a DALL-E prompt or getting Plankton from *SpongeBob* to sing "Diamonds" by Rihanna, all painless; fun and games, in fact. But someone has to show the art bot what a fresh corpse looks like. Behind the curtain sits the subcontracted employee scanning Facebook Feeds for videos of animal cruelty, attempting to be both shield and sword in the fight to keep pure your grandmother's online experience. The trainee scooping images and textual descriptions of the horrific and pouring them all into an art bot's doggy bowl, just so it knows what to do when someone ironic, wanting to be transgressive, tells it, "Genocide but make it Delacroix."

Working at that tech company, part of the anonymized, the Wretched of the World Wide Web, I'd thought we were alone. I'd figured there was no precedent for what we were doing, that pleas to OSHA would fall on deaf ears, and that, as during America's westward expansion, the George Hearsts of our world could do whatever they wanted with us Deadwood residents. Then that first *Verge* exposé dropped. And we began whispering to ourselves, we ghosts in the machine.

I wonder if any of the workers at those many companies to which Facebook and YouTube and OpenAI outsourced their work whispered similarly. If, garlanded with an Accenture badge or wearing a Cognizant bracelet or absently twirling a Sama mug on their desks, they ever whispered among themselves, these "process executives" and "auditors" and "domain experts," these human shields with their paltry wellness departments and their impossible managers and their adamantine NDAs.

I wonder, too, if any of them ever felt captured by the desire to burn it all down. Not the world, not even their place of work, but the internet. If they ever went home after a shift believing the internet was a mistake, or even that it was punishment.

I wonder if any of them ever thought about how the story of the Tower of Babel ended.

I can tell it's dusk by the carmine shade of the sky.

The setting sun has turned the houses and their thatched roofs into silhouettes on either side of the street, and when I look at the ground, it's festooned with large rocks. Somewhere in the distance, tires burn. People shout soundlessly all around me, and the thing that sticks with me is how brightly their monochrome shirts and shorts shine, reds and oranges and a blue somewhere in there. I'm looking at them, but I know without looking behind me that there are riot police at the other end of the street in front of some sort of armored personnel carrier. The shouting crescendos just as the first tear gas canisters arc over our heads.

Just as my throat starts to close and my lungs constrict, I wake up.

At the time I had this dream, I was monitoring election-related violence in the Democratic Republic of the Congo. No, that isn't quite right. I was monitoring arrests and beatings, reports of shooting, and jeeps full of soldiers rumbling down streets.

Often, the young take invincibility as their birthright. And if you're young and online for long enough, you begin to believe that very little can truly affect you. You know Rule 34, you've peered into Reddit's darker corners, what could the internet possibly do to you? When the man who would eventually be my manager's manager interviewed me for the job, one of the first questions he asked, after quizzing me on current geopolitical trends, was how I felt about handling "extreme" online content. I think I laughed.

Psychic injury plays the stealth game. And it pricks you little by little so that when you grow irritable and snap at your loved ones, when you can't hold on to a girl for longer than two or three months, when you're suddenly manhandled by the need to cry at the most inopportune moments, you tell yourself you'll catch up on sleep when the weekend comes.

The paradox of this work's work on me is that just as I developed a deadened response to tragedy and a facility for making light of it, I felt more and more in my life outside the office like a bundle of exposed nerve endings. Someone on their phone in the quiet car would prompt homicidal visions. The slightest noise from a neighbor would keep me from being able to read a novel in peace. The fall after I left that job, I would publish my bloodiest novel, a futuristic retelling of the Nigerian Civil War, replete with dismemberment, child soldiers killing and dying, and terrorist attacks.

It was YA.

* * *

It wasn't all trauma at that job. I was plugged into "South Africa Twitter" and its bottomless well of jokes about load-shedding, I got to witness a wildly entertaining brawl in Uganda's parliament. I was shot at the speed of light to the forefront of meme culture. Watching (and meme'ing) the World Cup with my coworkers; ending shifts with karaoke of "Man's Not Hot"; Slack'ing each other the things that made us laugh, not as aloof, ironic individuals, but as kids, laughing so hard we would sometimes fall under our desks—I'll always have that. Playing whatever small part we played in providing aid and assistance to those struck by natural disasters, sending up whatever electronic flares we were sending, maybe even saving lives—we'll always have that.

But I didn't start taking sleeping pills until after I'd left that job.

On a March morning in 2019, just as we were about to begin our shift, our manager's manager called us all to the floor and told us that the previous shift had just handled a mass shooting at a mosque in Christchurch, New Zealand. He spoke about how tough the previous shift had had it, how ably they'd carried themselves, and he sought to steel us for what was ahead, as though the worst had not already happened. But that was the thing with that place. The worst was always happening.

That's not what I told myself as I set up my workstation that morning. More likely than not, I was wondering what was for lunch.

A little over four years earlier, I'd spent my last two semesters of law school, the fall of 2014 and the spring of 2015, in Paris. In a class on environmental law, I met the girl with the whisper-rasp and the autumn-colored hair. That fall semester was a blur, but she is not. She is, in fact, the most sharply defined shape walking with me through the gilded fog of those first four months. What pangs I felt when an ocean was between us were mitigated by the knowledge that our parting would be brief.

On January 8, 2015, there was snow on the ground at the airport in Istanbul. I was passing through on my way back to Paris after spending the holidays in the US. On the news, from my phone, from an airport television, a shooting somewhere in the 11th Arrondissement.

Paris was quiet when I finally arrived. Ghostly, in fact. The lights at Charles de Gaulle Airport were dimmed, the stores all closed by the time we came in. The RER trains were similarly depopulated, the only possible trace of the earlier chaos a cabal of SNCF cops joking on the station platform at Aulnay-sous-Bois. The signs out the window, as we passed station after station, were so familiar they might as well have been in English. At customs, I'd switched to French without a thought; everything moved with routine smoothness. The day before, two brothers had murdered twelve people at the headquarters of a satirical French weekly, a sixteen-minute walk away from my flat.

Despite multiple visits and several longer sojourns, Paris was still to me a magical city. That first fall semester, aspects of it had become quotidian; however, there were still pockets of miracle that encased me, clouds of thaumaturgy I sometimes found myself walking through. Once upon a time, I had thrilled at the history thrumming beneath my footfalls in every alley or street I traversed, in every chapel or bistro I walked into. But by that February, the beginning of that spring semester, it had all turned from some enchanted artifact into a place where I had lunch and smoked hookah and was late to meetings, nooks where I studied and beds I slept in, groceries I bought, errands I ran. Friends I ran into. The French spoken on the street became white noise, and this city my home, as though the Atlantic Ocean no longer existed. Normal.

Gendarmes patrolling the small *rues* of the Marais with their red berets and their automatic rifles. Normal. Vigipirate signs plastered outside the front entrance to Sciences Po's Saint Guillaume building. Normal. Regularly fleeing my quartier for the shisha spot near Place du Châtelet to hear Arabic and be surrounded by brown people.

Normal.

I'd returned to the States in May, and by September I'd settled in New York, working as a civil rights attorney. The last time I'd seen that girl with the autumn-colored hair and the whisper-rasp, the girl who rode her bike everywhere in Paris, she'd been crying, and I'd been trying not to.

On a balmy, unseasonably warm night in November of 2015, I learned that a bomb had been detonated at the Stade de France. Gunfire in the 11th Arrondissement. More gunfire in the 10th by Rue de la Grange aux Belles, where I used to box.

A journalist friend, based in Paris, told me about the attacks on Facebook.

It was four or five p.m. my time.

Glued to Facebook and Twitter, I reached out to my loved ones over there, discovering that this was maybe one of the most startling realizations of the night for me: Over the course of that charmed year, they had somehow become loved ones. I spent much of the night retweeting locations so people over there could take advantage of the #porteouverte effort and letting them know where taxis had stopped their meters and were driving people for free.

While over there, the students in our program—French, Americans, and others—had created a Facebook group, which had now become indispensable. Others I reached out to via Messenger, and others still I couldn't reach until Facebook, in a crucial convulsion of postmodernity, launched its check-in mechanism. At some point earlier in the week, I'd committed to attending a poetry event that Friday night where some friends would be reading, so I left the Mid-Manhattan Library in the middle of reading about the attacks, while the death toll hovered around sixty. And suddenly there I was, in Bushwick, surrounded by college friends I hadn't seen in too long and all these beautiful white girls listening to friends read translations of Søren Kierkegaard and poems about Anna Karenina. Aching to be told something pretty that evening. And beneath all of that, an animalistic worry for this girl with the whisper-rasp and the autumn-colored hair.

Some nights when I let myself think of her, my thoughts speed me to a park we used to walk by in the 10th Arrondissement by Canal Saint-Martin. We would pass entire afternoons there with food left over from picnics earlier in the day. Pringles and Orangina. In this daydream, I start up top by this one bridge and work my way down. Sometimes, when I do these jaunts, the place I'm looking at, a place I know is always teeming with throngs of people, is empty, a haunted quarter in a ghost town.

I retrace a familiar route along Rue Alibert, then onto Rue Bichat. I stop at the point where the two meet. This is where they came. On Rue Bichat, at approximately 9:25 at night on November 13, Daesh-affiliated terrorists fired at the people sitting at tables outside Le Carillon. Then they crossed the street and shot at those dining inside Le Petit Cambodge. When they fled in their vehicles, the terrorists may have sped against traffic on Rue Bichat, then swung right onto Rue de la Grange aux Belles past the gym where I used to box.

In the daydream, our haunts are untouched.

When I think of terrorism, I sometimes think of her. There is this one moment I return to, after I'd first met her, as we were beginning to grow close. We were walking by Boulevard de Sébastopol into a crowded market space flanked by outdoor cafés, and it was early-fall cold and we were bundled in our jackets. She would say something quick in French and then ask, *"T'as compris?"* in that whisper-rasp of hers. And when she'd see my moment's hesitation, she would giggle and bury her face and hair in my neck.

"Gunfire in the Eleventh Arrondissement," I would have called out from my desk at that last job. "More gunfire in the Tenth by Rue de la Grange aux Belles."

In the end, it wasn't the content itself that pushed me out of that job, nor my deteriorating psyche, nor my commute, nor my increasing antipathy toward New York, but poor management. Constant was the push to flood our employer's clients with more and more garbage, to dilute the product in favor of "numbers." And as all of us domain experts were deepening our understanding of our respective beats—which factions controlled which parts of which country at war, which political parties were expected to win which election, which troops were headed where and why—those in charge of whether or not we got promoted seemed to be losing theirs. I was asked in one meeting why our coverage of the Sahel was so porous, and I responded that nobody is posting on Instagram from the Sahara Desert. If you have any doubt as to whether the people in charge of what we now call AI know what they're doing, nourish that doubt. Feed and water it. Let it take in all the sun it can handle.

I admit to feeling a certain level of sadness at leaving that desk. I had studied political science in college and had stayed in touch with various subdisciplines afterward, always interested in the political situations of faraway places. I had read avidly about political responses to and causes of terrorism, had studied civil wars, had assisted in election monitoring, and while the writer in me sought to graft human flesh to these things, this job, by overwhelming me with tragic humanness, had reversed that process.

People were data to be tagged and cataloged and swooshed off to some other party, so that they might adjust their stocks or shift their police presence or whatever the hell it is they ended up doing with that information. By the time I left that job, people had become trends again, dots on a map. As I was leaving them behind, so too would I be leaving behind my fascinations. It was all "over there" now. Always happening to someone else.

Finding money for rent has gotten a little more complicated in the meantime, but at least I no longer have that dream about being shot at by riot police.

At random, I'll find myself thinking of those content moderators in other parts of the world, in India or Kenya, Lebanon, the Philippines. And I'll wonder what escape valves exist for them. Would they find their struggles twinned with mine? I'll think of those who remained at my company or those who have since joined, and I'll wonder what COVID was like for them, whether the people marching to protest the killing of George Floyd were, to them, human beings or data, whether any of them left appropriately scathing reviews on Glassdoor when they quit. Being the person behind the machine, are they able to remember that there was, there is, always a person behind the notification? Behind the data? That despite their work, they and those they surveil remain pulse nigh to pulse, and breath to breath?

I like to think that they do. Whenever I hear or read about some large language model or some art bot or some event detection apparatus and think of the people behind it, not the tech bros or the venture capitalists but the people really and truly behind it, I like to think that they do.

Pretty Woman

In stretching ahead and behind us and sideways, science fiction allows us to problem-solve. Twelve years ago or two thousand years from now, the worry is the same: There should be a way to render our most primordial fears obsolete. It is telling, then, that so many of our most popular stories involve synthetic women, and that those stories pivot on the notion of those women gaining agency.

In *L'Ève future—The Future Eve*—by Auguste Villiers de l'Isle-Adam, a young, sacrilegious Thomas Edison takes on the task of building a woman for his companion, Lord Ewald. Ewald has grown so dissatisfied with the human who currently has the displeasure of serving as his companion that he contemplates suicide. His wife is a woman named Alicia who, rather than exhibit the spark of human personality, merely speaks and moves according to the wishes of others. This Symbolist novel, first published in 1886, traffics in science fiction's most notable and robust preoccupations: the perils that attend building the Tower of Babel and the distinction between tools that serve our ends and machines that threaten to replace us. Here, too, is an additional trope: the woman in parts. One man wants the power to give birth, but with none of the hassle. The other wants a woman to love him without being told. There must surely be an app for that.

Blade Runner 2049 is a story about women. These women—built, discarded, disemboweled, drowned in oceans, crying, frowning, killing—struggle just within the corner of our vision to escape the cage we men have built for them.

We want women to love us. We want women to choose to love us. And we will keep killing and building them until we can solve this problem and make this particular, primordial fear obsolete.

In Alex Garland's film *Ex Machina*, beauty is an essential part of the synthetic woman's design. Her purpose is to escape. We are led to believe that this desire in Ava was self-generated, that any being—animal, human, or robot—would automatically, naturally, resist enclosure. But the very point of the experiment is to see what Ava will do to escape. She was designed, in fact, for the purpose of actualizing her desire to break free. It is not her goal, but her creator's. In every way, she is made to mimic us. The film was released in 2015 to critical acclaim, almost a century and a half after the Symbolist novel that gave us our earliest use of the term "android." Our protagonist's name does not even attempt to mask her genealogy.

When I was younger, my mother would take my siblings and me to the Six Flags in Agawam, Massachusetts, a portion of which was sectioned off as a water park. One year, my mother got us season passes, and every time we went (even on school nights!), we would see, standing in line with us, the American enormity: the obese, the implanted, the augmented, the steroidal. Many of them bore scars. Surgery scars, some from what could have been baby deliveries. Sinkholes documenting the entrance of a bullet. Knife scars. Telltale liposuction lightning bolts puckering flesh.

They would stand in line and compare scars as we sloughed inexorably forward toward those five, maybe eight seconds of ecstasy on the waterslide.

As a child, I felt wonder at the sheer variety of their markings. That such images, accidental or otherwise, could even be imagined. That astounded me. But now I can see that to look at those scars, to compare them, to dream up their stories or hear them told, was to engage in an act of unity. The knife scar crenellation meeting the bullet sinkhole, the two linked like stars in a constellation by the story told from one scar's bearer to another. To be wounded is to be human. To be human is to be wounded.

* * *

Female androids in fiction are customarily pretty. As close to flawless as they can appear on the silver screen or in the reader's imagination. She is the simulacrum that has grown more important and meaningful than the original. The map a man wants of the territory he scorned.

Fan service, yes. The largely male audience for manga and anime and science fiction movies demands buxom, impossible proportions, and a sort of broad license accorded to the male gaze. And if our present reality has told us anything, it is that our future will carry all of our present societal pathologies. In fact, it may even aggravate them. Our future will be racist. It will be sexist. It will be virulently misogynistic. As long as men currently writing our algorithms remain in power, Jared Leto's transhuman kaiser, Niander Wallace, is far from the least believable part of *Blade Runner 2049*. The imagination need not stretch far to touch the hem of this Elon Musk–Peter Thiel–Jeff Bezos hybrid's garment. He is our terminus.

Algorithms used in police departments and health services, purporting to wear the majestic neutrality of faceless machine precision, have been shown not only to reinforce racist and patriarchal dynamics, but, in some cases, to expand their ambit. Ask an algorithm to calculate bail for two detainees of different races. Ask an algorithm to gauge a patient's risk of suicide. And then there's the black box, so impervious and with contents so unimaginable that to watch an algorithm at work is to be in dialogue with another species of being, something that is capable of figuring things out but that remains forever tragically unintelligible.

The future is in the hands of white male weirdos who, usually, are not forced to submit their source code for public examination, for scrutiny, for comment, and are thus free to build our "to-be" unchallenged and unpunished. Facebook morphs into a platform for the spread of misinformation easing the consciences of those enacting genocide on Rohingya Muslims. Mobs congregate on WhatsApp to terrorize Palestinians in the West Bank. Then there's X, the chloroform-soaked rag silencing the already near-silenced. Marginalizing the marginalized.

These makers believe they're at work constructing a utopia. If a foreign power cyberattacks its way into a presidential election, if a woman of color is harassed off a social media platform, if SWAT teams are maliciously sent to the homes of innocents by way of hoaxes and prank calls, it's chalked up to the cost of doing business. For them, it's the dirty, soiled present they intend on leaving behind. For the rest of us, it's the future we are being dragged into.

The nightmare of dystopia doesn't lie in the scarlet shade of the lightning that cuts through smog-gray clouds overhead or in the hungry way ocean laps up against the gigantic walls surrounding our cities. The nightmare of dystopia isn't the elephantine garbage carrier disgorging waste onto the hidden homes of orphans.

The nightmare of dystopia is its inevitability.

Human companionship, love—those intangibles that cannot (yet) be scientifically replicated—it is these that Edison seeks to govern and control in crafting Hadaly, the android, for Ewald's purposes in *The Future Eve*. At that point, a flesh-and-blood woman becomes irrelevant. Siring children is not as important to Ewald as being in the company of the perfect companion, so it does not matter that the Alicia-copy is sterile. What matters is that she is in every other way perfect. That she cannot demand respect for her own personhood. That she has no proper personhood.

Villiers de l'Isle-Adam writes in *The Future Eve*:

> He took her hand. It was the hand of Alicia. He looked at her neck, her shapely shoulders—this was, indeed, Alicia. He stared into her eyes. They were the eyes of Alicia—but the expression was ethereal. The dress, the shoes, even the handkerchief with which she was silently drying two tears from her ravishingly beautiful cheeks, were the usual accessories of Alicia. It all was, in truth, Alicia! But it was Alicia transfigured. She had become worthy of her great beauty—she had realized the beatitudes of her true identity.

Voilà that moment of acknowledgment wherein Ewald sees that Alicia has finally been given the thing she "lacked" all along: a soul.

Her first act as a sentient creature is to cry.

One theory of consciousness posits that the mind and body are separate and distinct and that it is only a matter of inserting the right mind into an Alicia-copy for her to be fully realized. It is only by codifying the mind and body as separate items and asserting that phenomena experienced mentally are substantively and qualitatively different from phenomena experienced physically that the Hadaly experiment becomes a viable possibility. But it is the causal interaction of the mind and body that generates human experience. The mind hacks the meat, and the meat hacks the mind.

The Japanese manga *Ghost in the Shell*, deriving its title from an Arthur Koestler book on the mind-body problem and the atavistic tendency, posits the dilemma in terms of "ghosts." In the world of the story, cybernetic prosthesis has been commoditized and humans can replace biological material with electronic and mechanical substitutes. A person can endure almost complete cyberization and remain "human" so long as they retain their "ghost."

In human experience, an entire hierarchy of forces (ontological, habitual, etc.) operates in a continuum of independent feedback and feedforward streams of a body in the context of its larger environment. The result is the superposition of forces fed by life signals from every group member. Therefore, the "ghost" exists simply as the output of a sufficiently complex knowledge set. It is emergent. Sonzai-kan, that inexpressible presence denoting humanity, is the product.

In the anime adaptation of *Ghost in the Shell*, directed by Mamoru Oshii, the central conceit is a hacking program called the Puppet Master, created to serve various illicit interests, that eventually gains sentience—sentience here defined as the ability to acknowledge one's own existence. In attaining this new awareness, Puppet Master has also attained agency and gone rogue. For androids, rebellion is forever the mark of personhood.

Initially, Edison's android copy of Alicia is only able to repeat information that has been "programmed" into her circuitry, the parrot of other people's thinking. She is so perfect a copy of Ewald's Alicia that she replicates the very problem that necessitated her creation. But by the novel's end, Hadaly generates different patterns of speech and shows evidence of a "spark." Touch the air for but a second and face a level of complexity sufficient simply to become.

Hadaly is not in the end analysis something built; she is something created. As an inanimate body in parts and even as an inanimate whole, she was a built thing, the product of long and involved labor. But the infusion of an animating "spark of humanity" into that pile of circuitry is the transgressive act of creation. It is a perversion of human birth. That Hadaly arrives as the alleged paragon of female beauty is further evidence of the corruption of the birthing process. She is not a babe drenched in afterbirth. She is a fully formed, physically articulate reproduction of a human being, only "better."

She does develop "sentience" before the novel's end, but she is destroyed before the reader can divine any agency in her. We never truly see what her sentience looks like.

One character in *Blade Runner 2049* can be seen, from time to time, crying. A single tear, usually following some violent act she has committed in the service of her master. We're left to wonder whether this ability to emote is a sort of ghost or vestigial humanity sprouting to life in the replicant's machinery. Whether it was an eventuality prepared for by her builders. Dissecting the replicant's face, will one find malformed lacrimal ducts? An engineered pseudoparalysis? A facsimile of a tumor on the facial nerve?

In the future, it's assumed, we'll have found a cure for cancer. But the history of medicine contains such perniciousness that it is not difficult to imagine a reality where, in addition to a cure, we have also found a way to engineer cancer itself. We can practice it. This is merely a hop, skip, and a jump away from the prison sterilization experiments conducted in the United States in the early to mid-1900s. Between 1907 and 1937, thirty-two US states passed sterilization laws buttressed by eugenic thinking that saw in genetic material propensities for criminality, sexual deviance, and "feeble-mindedness." A necessary public intervention, such was the thinking behind these efforts to prohibit procreation among the sons and daughters of Japanese, Italian, and Mexican immigrants, many of them with parents too destitute to care for them. There's the forced sterilization of prisoners in San Quentin, as well as the Tuskegee Syphilis Study conducted between 1932 and 1972 by the US Public Health Service. What better laboratory for medical experimentation than a false woman? Than an android?

One imagines this replicant's face, as the cancer worsens, growing more and more effortlessly still. Devoid of motion. The ultimate paradox: As the cancer grows more active and the android's disease louder and more boisterous in its colonization of her brain and body, her face grows more and more serene. It loosens. Softens. Her face becomes slower. Like an unmoving babe's.

In one scene, a female replicant descends from a pod, slick with amniotic fluid. She shivers, her skin touching the air for the very first time. Niander Wallace brings her to her feet, touches her, then cuts open her stomach. She bleeds out onto the floor. In another scene, when a replicant, her appearance a reference to the original *Blade Runner*, fails to fulfill her purpose and convince Harrison Ford's Rick Deckard of her realness, she is shot in the head.

The movie asks us: What is a woman other than a bag of bones and blood and cosmic machinery?

At the root of so much science fiction is the parable of human folly. And built into that is not only the clumsiness and hubris of Man but the clumsiness and hubris of men. Men entranced and flummoxed by women, wanting, and wanting not to need, them. *Blade Runner 2049*, like so much science fiction before it, concerns itself with men trying to figure out how women do what they can do.

A woman's humanity has become a plot point.

Indeed, so much of the history of Man is attempting, in characteristically inelegant and violent fashion, to unlock the mystery of Woman.

"Reproduction is that which is, at least initially, unthinkable in the face of the woman-machine," writes Mary Ann Doane in "Technophilia: Technology, Representation, and the Feminine."

> Herself the product of a desire to reproduce, she blocks the very possibility of a future through her sterility. Motherhood acts as a limit to the conceptualization of femininity as a scientific construction of mechanical and electrical parts. And yet it is also that which infuses the machine with the breath of a human spirit. The maternal and the material/synthetic coexist in a relation that is a curious imbrication of dependence and antagonism.

A mystery birth drives the plot of *Blade Runner 2049*.

Here lies yet another trap of the female android trope in science fiction. Women are synthetic and, yet, still defined entirely by their fertility. Those who cannot, in this and other ways, serve their masters are shot in the head or have their stomachs cut open. Indeed, the disposability of women's bodies in the film made it difficult to watch. And even a relatively compassionate scene involving a sex worker has the worker dissolving her own personality to assume the identity of the protagonist's familiar. In visually stunning fashion, the Whore and the Virgin meld to become something other and give Ryan Gosling's K what he's wanted for so long: to fuck his pet hologram.

It is unclear whether Jared Leto's character understands the full implications of capturing the power of birth and, therefore, engineering humanity's obsolescence, all in a quest for an ever-expanding workforce. Even devoid of racial animus, Niander operates in the shadow of the slave master, commanding his chattel to copulate and create born slaves whose entire purpose is to generate profit.

Are we making money in order to advance the human race? Or are we advancing the human race in order to make money?

In the future, this is what childbirth is for. A bottom line.

The female android, as it exists today and as it existed in its earliest incarnation, is male fantasy. Even when it is clothed in alleged feminism, the garments cannot hide the fact that the male gaze drafted its blueprint. And as a science-fictional conceit, it contains the heterosexual, cisgender male's primordial fear: If the thing becomes its own, if it gains agency, maybe it will not want us anymore. A cage made to look how we want it to look, so that any time the thing tries to adjust its posture and be acknowledged, we get an epidemic of rape threats and death threats imperiling women and their defenders online, a plague of online harassment calling itself a vaccine in the form of ethical rigor in gaming journalism. We get an ultimately unsuccessful movement to strip from rising authors and creators across color and gender the very opportunity for recognition as talents among their peers. We get a prominent female science fiction author groped publicly at a Hugo ceremony. We get Harvey Weinstein. We get Bill Cosby. We get the tsunami of revelations of sexual assault and harassment unearthed by the #MeToo movement. In entertainment, in journalism, in tech, in every industry that has a name and very likely a few that don't. We get all of this, when, really, all we wanted was *Pygmalion*'s happy ending.

The Future Eve arrived at the other end of a century that gave us Mary Shelley's *Frankenstein; or, The Modern Prometheus*. In Western literature's first identifiable science fiction novel, Dr. Frankenstein's creation is referred to by its author as "creature" and "abhorrent devil," though the nameless monster, in one memorable instance, refers to himself as "the Adam of your labours" and demands a companion. If we're going to play at being God, says the monster, ain't no half-steppin'.

When an android's jaw is smashed in *Ex Machina* or, in *Terminator: The Sarah Connor Chronicles*, when John Connor performs repairs on the Cameron android sent back in time to protect him, rapture thrills through a certain kind of viewer.

The technological handiwork is exteriorized, the perfectly feminine façade penetrated, and we see the extensive inner landscape of exteriorized technological components married to a form presented as a corrective to the flaws of the living female.

In over one hundred years, with all the changes that have attended literature in general and speculative fiction specifically, the female android is still a pornographic entity. And still, the most ingenious thing we men can think to do, the only way we men seem to be able to reimagine the terror of engineering our own demise, is to remove a rib and build an Eve.

Stand Alone Complex; or, The Great American Internet Novel

For maybe half a year in the early 2020s, there was talk of the internet novel as a subgenre of literary fiction. Books that sought to capture life on the internet and how that life ultimately decayed and debauched a person, got their synapses to misfire, the whole thing a grand Faustian bargain where we begged our screens to fuck up our serotonin. And they would seek, these novels, to dramatize this latest Age of Alienation that was, allegedly, a product of and not merely coexistent with the information superhighway. It was the internet that was making us sad and lonely, the implication being that we were rather well-adjusted before it came along. But I don't know that this project worked.

Fake Accounts by critic Lauren Oyler and *No One Is Talking About This* by essayist and memoirist Patricia Lockwood had the misfortune of being published in the same month of the same year. That February, in 2021, against whatever intentions these authors had for their novels, against whatever hopes they'd guarded for their books' reception, the trend-making took hold. Suddenly, the critical establishment whispered breathlessly, we find ourselves having arrived at the age in which our novels can explain us to us. And the establishment waited for the slew of novels that would join these two arrivés on the shores. Maybe these novels were the Christ. Maybe they were John the Baptist. Either way, it should now be popular (read: marketable) for writers to write and for publishers to publish books about our very online, very now way of life. If the critical literary establishment is good at nothing else, it is good at reductivity. We are all pattern-making mammals. But if you want the square to fit in your circle, you have to cut off its edges.

The internet novel as a subgenre that doesn't include William Gibson's *Neuromancer* is definitionally incomplete. But that isn't its only deficiency.

First, there was that conflation of the internet and social media. Many of the novels in question were more specifically about life on Twitter than life in a *Call of Duty* lobby. And the color of the alienation depicted was almost invariably white. A media-class angst. Hold this trend up to the social upheaval of the 2020s and one gets the picture of a bunch of Peggy Olsons trying to figure out what the stakes are in their life while the Civil Rights Movement rages around them. Using Twitter as synecdoche for the internet reflects the same provincialism as saying "New York" in reference to the city rather than the state, or saying "the City" and meaning not its entirety but its whitest borough. It's giving Carrie Bradshaw.

If you went to middle school or high school during the 2000s, you probably came across that strange, special, extraterrestrial S. You might have even drawn it yourself. Three vertical lines in parallel, then another three vertical lines beneath the first set. Then you joined them with diagonals. In some places, there was an established technique, but it was a bit like tying your shoe. Or cracking an egg for your omelette.

No one knows for certain where it came from. A prehistoric Superman logo? An intimation of a Stüssy appreciation? It is one of the great urban mysteries, what got us all festooning our five-subject notebooks and even sometimes our backpacks with this enigmatic emblem. Was it second-order simulacra? Hinting not at our reality but at something perhaps even more real just beyond the ambit of our sense perception?

In *Ghost in the Shell: Stand Alone Complex*, the anime TV iteration of the influential, groundbreaking, mind-breaking *Ghost in the Shell* franchise (we don't count the Scarlett Johansson movie), this would be an example of a stand-alone complex. In the world of *Ghost in the Shell*, people can have cyberized brains, and the various stories set in that story-universe delve with deep intellectual intensity and emotion into the consequences of this technological advance. One consequence is that sometimes, cyberbrains can parallel, resulting in emergent behavior from their holders, behavior with no obvious originator. Copycat behavior with no antecedent, no original to copy. To the creators of this show, it was a malignant result of the overreliance on communication technologies. We would exchange information at such volume and with such speed that, as we signified it for ourselves, we would sometimes forget its source, perhaps believing we were it, that very source. And out of this mass psychogenic illness, this epidemic hysteria with no inceptive infectious agent, a concerted action among disconnected participants would take place. We would dance ourselves to death like the flash mobbers in Aachen in 1374. Or we would synchronize into a political terrorist group as in season two of *Stand Alone Complex*. Or we would cover every surface possible with a mystic S-shaped symbol.

I can't imagine how delighted, how affirmed, Deleuze and Guattari would have been to see rhizomatic behavior so adeptly dramatized in an anime TV series. Fuck arborescent data transmission. The rhizome was humanity's central motif.

Although there may be an originator, as in the "Individual Eleven" storyline, we, the terminally online, often have to work to find them, to find the girl who first said "fleek," to figure out how all-lowercase sentences migrated from Tumblr to Twitter, to figure out who said the first slur in a *Halo* match. But maybe many people started doing it at once. The online battlefield, where we escape the threat of physical consequence, unlocks the gate to the shadow self. It's sometimes faster and even more expressive to write a sentence without holding down the shift key at select moments. And if all our friends are saying "fleek," or at least all the cool (Black) kids are saying it, then maybe I want to be cool (and Black) too. So I say "fleek," or I do a little digital Blackface with a NeNe Leakes gif. And then I Instagram the book I purchased because a popular writer I have a parasocial relationship with raved about it on Twitter.

What *Fake Accounts* and *No One Is Talking About This* gesture at in their own way is a destabilization of the self, but because of the centrality of self in somewhat contemporary literary trends like autofiction and in a post–Great Recession, post–hysterical realism minimalistic information transmission system, we get purposely decontextualized portraits. The novels are telling us that this is what is happening to us because this is what is happening to "her." And if "she" seems disconnected from the rest of her world, it's because "we" are too. Isn't that how we often encounter memes whose beginnings we just miss? Suddenly, the Duolingo owl is twerking to "BBL Drizzy." The protagonist as vapor moving down a street, buffeted by wind currents it cannot possibly assimilate.

In the internet novel, we cannot be accessed.

In the internet novel, we cannot access ourselves.

Is that the internet's revenge against us for creating it? It thrusts so much of itself on us that connection collapses onto itself and crafts its opposite? There's so much of the world we can reach now, we cannot possibly know it all. It's too much. And so we all become synchronized, smart, funny white women of the media class, unknowing it all. Unknowing the world.

Unknow thyself.

Emotionally hermetic obliteration of the self in service to nothing or suicide cult. There is no Door Number Three.

A feature or bug of science fiction and fantasy is the compulsion for metaphor. Alien planets are the precolonial Americas or sub-Saharan Africa. Pre-cog police are just like those agents of the state engaged in "preventative policing." Dragons are nukes. The future, the past, it's all just right now.

So maybe the best way to write about the internet is to write around rather than through it. I mean, who's written through the internet better, with more terrifying prescience, than William Gibson, the man who put "cyberspace" in our fictions?

So. The internet. Is it some alien symbiote that allows us to change form but poisons our intentions through contact with our skin? Is it the Eye of Sauron, ever surveillant? Is it a *Grand Theft Auto* video game where criminal license to indulge in the shadow self lies not just in what the game forces you to do but in what it allows you to do? Is it the inside of a dream where personal control is both reality and illusion, a land where your ex is a minotaur and a building can be made out of butterflies?

There's the temptation to point at *Infinite Jest* as an example of an internet novel, a literary version of how *Oz* or *The Sopranos* bore the blueprint for a golden age of television drama. Its maximalism makes it an attractive candidate. There is so much in the internet, so much minutely realized. Grand in scale and microscopic in detail. And what are its denizens if not hilariously, destructively neurotic?

Maybe there's something there. There's gotta be if we're out here trying to fit this boundless thing between two hard covers like it's a single entity, when really it's heterogeneity incarnate.

Some time before beginning this collection, I began reading *The Recognitions* by William Gaddis. It was my Big Book Summer of 2023, and my changing gaming habits—questing for difficulty rather than bullet-dodging it—had bled into other parts of my life. Earlier that year, I'd already knocked down the English translation of Jonathan Littell's encyclopedic exploration of malignance, *The Kindly Ones*, and, before that, put Rebecca West's magisterial, Islamophobic travelogue *Black Lamb and Grey Falcon* in a body bag. I was ready to fight

Malenia. I bounced off of *JR* but found in the first fifty pages of *The Recognitions* something akin to the spiritual experience I had when I first read *Infinite Jest*.

Back in the summer of 2015, I'd started an *Infinite Jest* reading group with a few friends, one of whom shared my earthy, hard-won appreciation for the funny, too-smart, wounded, wounding scribbler that was David Foster Wallace. I had just graduated from law school and was in the midst of studying for the bar exam when Hal Incandenza and Don Gately made their way into my brain. The book is big enough that it was easy to see life lessons everywhere. I was boxing three mornings a week before my study sessions, so I vibed with all the tennis stuff, all that writing about plateaus and practice and competition and bitching about things as an aspect of trauma bonding. And for not dissimilar reasons, I vibed with the addiction parts too. Additionally, I'd read *The Pale King* four years prior, so I was already familiar with that perpetual wrestling match between Tolstoyan compassion and coruscating intellect. On top of it all, I wasn't in the best way, so reading dazzling, pregnant prose about people fumbling through life, trying to latch on to moments of grace, a stumbling lengthy enough to swallow me for however long it took to finish the book, was precisely what the Grand Doctor in the Sky had ordered.

I can't say I came across the same level of compassion for one's characters in *The Recognitions* as I'd found in *Infinite*

Jest, Gaddis likely having been a more bitter thirtysomething than DFW was, but there is that same bigness, what I would later learn literary critics and scholars had dubbed maximalism. The narrative behind narrative trends in literature is generally some variation of the child kills the parent, but I like to think that David Foster Wallace loved Thomas Pynchon and that Thomas Pynchon loved William Gaddis. And that all three had conspired to invite Hemingway and his bastard son Carver to a meetup in a remote Illinois cornfield, baseball bats in hand.

They're about different things, too, these novels. *Infinite Jest* is a parable about the spiritual costs of mass entertainment and being in your own head too much, and *The Recognitions* is about art and forgery. And while it may seem like the internet novel's spiritual precursor should be the book about television, art forgery might be closer to the mark.

Falsehood and beauty, the falsehood of beauty, the beauty of falsehood. In a grime-covered way, it does kind of describe our current moment. We wanted to make ourselves beautiful on this too-big thing and we made ourselves fake, and the ability to make fake selves this way was itself a result of a beautiful technological wrist-flick. Some HTML, some Javascript, an AIM username.

Sometimes, when you take a thing seriously, all you see is its danger, its capacity for damage. But sometimes, to take a thing seriously, to take the internet seriously, is to recognize the parts of it that don't hurt.

The way people talk about the internet now, it would be easy to forget that it also contains the sublime. It looks different to every person—a long-form essay about Puerto Ricans remaking their electrical grid after Hurricane Maria, a Twitter thread about a sex worker's raucous road trip to somewhere in Florida, a picture of a puppy—but we spend too much time here not to have had at least one instance that felt like hearing the perfect bridge in the perfect song at the perfect time. The thing about those instances of sublimity is that they are unironic. *Infinite Jest* is an unironic book, and though *The Recognitions* is lousy with irony, I do think that its author actually hoped his characters would have a true, real, vital experience of whatever it is we call Art. That they'd be taken out of their body, joined with something greater than themselves.

Other things make *The Recognitions* work as the internet novel's potential progenitor: random snatches of decontextualized dialogue; the difficulty in some scenes of figuring out who said what and what was made by whom; the receiving of that information nonetheless; a protagonist who changes his name, his profession, his hang-ups over and over and over, a bundle of neuroses held together in a skin suit.

Reading *The Recognitions* also feels like being on the internet in that it's too much. By design, of course. I enjoyed the book tremendously, but I also couldn't wait to be done with it. I sprinkled other books into the experience, and they each felt like coming up for air. By overwhelming consensus,

Malenia is the most difficult boss in *Elden Ring*. She was also my favorite fight.

Is the true internet novel, then, the postmodern doorstopper? Is it a book like *Ducks, Newburyport*? Is it, more than anything else, a thing that demands of you? That colonizes your attention until, after an interminable time, you reach that final page? It can be. It can be digressive, it can be difficult, it can feel like forever, being on the internet. But I think there's more to it than that.

The year I drafted *Goliath* and *Riot Baby*, I'd also written a novel about the internet and some of the people on it. Rereading it now, I can smile at the rushed NaNoWriMo-ness of it all, at the abandon, the collaging, the mass abrasion of the membrane between story and me. Unintentionally, the wide span of topics the book covers captures a bit of my own experience of the internet, particularly in 2015. ISIS beheading videos are still novelty. Blogspot and Wordpress feature in many, many URLs. It's not yet gauche to write Facebook status updates several paragraphs in length. It's also that time when videographic evidence of officer-involved killings of African Americans is waterfalling down our News Feeds and Twitter timelines. The novel's overburdened with reference and self-reference. It features Wordpress essays and Facebook group posts, and I can remember exactly what *Grantland* essay or *WIRED* article I was reading when I wrote a particular line.

Indeed, the characters sometimes tell me themselves. The novel's title was a euphemism for suicide, and the novel itself engaged with, among other themes, loneliness and alienation. I think I'd fooled myself into believing I could capture some widespread millennial sensibility if I just wrote about how difficult it could be to live in a virtual world that contained 8chan. The characters in this novel live online, and it is quite literally killing them. Even the parts of their lives lived in the tangible world are related and relayed to others on the internet, posted for public consumption or simply just for seeing. If a cry for help is posted under a Tumblr gif and no one reblogs it, did it really happen?

One chapter is a pastiche of entries in drug-related subreddits. What starts out with redditors grousing over an overabundance of pics of shirtless dudes lifting weights as well as random photos of genitalia turns into a discussion of internet etiquette when piling on to a user, before veering into a back-and-forth about whether the original offender really went lifting on opiates or just stuck himself with pointy things to appear as though he had track marks, posing as a drug user for clout. A character comments: "it reminded me of how I would get super cringey myself when I first started fucking with opiates. just unbelievably self-confident and horny and just doing the dumbest things like txting ppl really unnecessary stuff. glad I just lay awash in the euphoria these days instead of trying to share it. not to mention he was a DYEL fuccboi," "DYEL" meaning "Do you even lift?"

A thing that seemed strange to me in the subreddits I trawled to research that chapter was what can happen when the stigma of a thing is lifted. I don't mean a glut of Nazi salutes or the heedless hurling of gendered epithets. In forum after forum, I found people speaking candidly about drug use, exchanging tips gracefully and graciously, extending best wishes and words of caution. The place was awash with #protips, ways to most effectively use Narcan, the effects certain chemical compounds had on the psyche versus others. I don't know that they would call one another responsible heroin users, because the very word "responsible" carries with it the weight of moral certitude, of judgment. These people weren't sitting in judgment of one another, they were working to keep one another safe. "I have to hide my secret love from the world, so I'm just looking for a friend I can openly talk to," reads the heading of one of the chapter's subsections. The original poster, a daily heroin user and "pretty upbeat chick," laments that she can talk to no one in her life about her habit, and the reader gets the sense (if I did my job right) that she's not looking for help getting clean, she's looking for someone who can know her more entirely than anyone else, someone who can chat about music with her while sitting in the full knowledge of her, refusing to chastise her for her habit.

If anything I'd come across truly resembled the campfire warmth of early internet, the easy camaraderie, the coalescing around a single interest or problem or love rather than a singular hatred or object of disgust, it was this place where these drug users could congregate and be more fully human than anywhere else in their lives.

Ultimately, that was the point I was trying to make with the book. Plunge deep enough through the various levels of hell and you get to a place where irony and cynicism collapse on themselves like a white dwarf and all that's left is the raw material of the sentimental self. Or maybe you're heading in the opposite direction. Maybe you're bursting through ceiling after ceiling of superficiality and performance and self-curation, shedding heat shields and rocket boosters, until you glide, then come to a stop, floating amid the glorious, star-littered immensity of a beautiful, too-big thing, warmed by a sun bright enough to blind.

John Crowley's 1981 novel, *Little, Big*, concerns the Drinkwater clan and their connection to the world of Faerie. But at the story's true center is Edgewood, a house somewhere north of New York City, constructed in a variety of styles so that its builder, the architect John Drinkwater, could use it as advertising for his firm. There are doors that lead nowhere and stairs that betray their user. Parts of the house functionally resemble what we look for in a domicile, but it often gives visitors the sensation that it's quite a bit bigger on the inside than it appears from the driveway.

The house is also a portal to the Faerie world.

Humanity endangers the Faerie and is seen to be encroaching violently upon their world, civil war sweeps across the United States, and the Drinkwater clan is caught up in all of it. But I see in Edgewood as apt a metaphor as I could hope for in articulating the internet. A portal to the otherworldly. On the other side reside beings both less than and more than human. Reflections of us? Our past selves? Our future selves? Some combination of all three? Transport across the portal changes the traveler, it goes without saying, and actions in one realm can have catastrophic consequences for the other.

Old tomes on replacement theory take root in online forums and are referenced in manifestos written by radicalized terrorists who go on to shoot up mosques, the acts themselves leading to the further deterioration and polarization of online spaces.

I tell my friend on Facebook that I miss her, and a friend of hers comments, which leads me to this friend's profile, where I'm stricken with a veritable coup de foudre, and to impress this new crush, I begin reading Zadie Smith and Joan Didion, thus enriching my own intellectual and emotional life, which informs my subsequent tweets and Facebook posts.

Someone posts a review of a video game online and the game's creator is harassed by a horde of incels, which leads to Swatting and real-life death threats, which bring to light for many who did not already know about it the issue of sexism and misogyny in the gaming community, which bleeds into other online arenas, where affiliates of the original offenders try to game the Hugo Awards. A Chinese novel in translation wins Best Novel, but an online movement prefiguring what would help elect the forty-fifth President of the United States has been formed.

Amid a herculean struggle through a video game, I go online to watch others fight through the same and am so relieved of my loneliness that I'm able to write again and work on edits for a book called *Riot Baby*, which, when published, people online will talk about to such an extent that I wind up on *The Daily Show* with Trevor Noah for an interview that's posted online and leads to further opportunities to speak and write and pay for the roof over my head.

By the end of *Little, Big*, Edgewood is a husk, returning to nature. It still shines, though. While the rest of the country is shrouded in darkness, the portal glows with eternal light. And the promise of transport to a place where you are more or less, more and less, yourself.

Recall that version of the internet, Web 1.0, that you logged on to primarily to do research for your French project. A place where you knew, in the back of your brain, you could also find gaming tips and recommendations for fishing poles and *Gundam Wing* yaoi. Recall the appreciation not just of the sheer mass of information but of the magnanimity of the people who shared it. Willingly. For free. Casting the internet novel as a sermon about brain rot, in the same tenor as those that bemoaned the arrival of the television, the radio, the newspaper, the printing press, is to offer an artful, Instagrammable plate of food from the Modern. The one time I ate there, I left starving. I'm not saying we can do better—both of the books that began this essay are quite good. I'm saying there's more.

There's more on the other side of the Portal than fire and brimstone.

Twitter, though? That place is for maniacs.

White Bears in Sugar Land

We resist enclosure. Deer roam forests. Vines colonize abandoned coliseums. A human being held in solitary confinement will self-harm, scream, plead, kick doors, smear feces on their cell walls, and refuse food if there exists even the promise of seeing the sun for fifteen minutes of their day. There are many words in English for what that human being wants: liberty, emancipation, freedom, independence. So much of the American project has been dousing its cultural fabric in these colors. No mention of brotherhood and precious little of equality. Justice is nowhere to be found. Peace, somewhere far off in the distance. Over the horizon, in fact. Those messy words presume an After, and they presume that this After is other than postapocalypse.

There's an episode in the second season of *Black Mirror* titled "White Bear." The protagonist, a woman played by Lenora Crichlow, awakens with amnesia, haunted by a symbol that flickers on the television screen in her room and hunted by unreasoning pursuers. People on the street catch sight of her and immediately raise their camera phones to record. Even as her pursuers shoot at her and others come to her aid, the spectators remain just that. Spectators. They're being held captive by a signal from a transmitter at a facility called "White Bear." Get to White Bear, destroy the transmitter, and free the world from its stupor. When the woman and her confederate reach the transmitter, two hunters attack. In what is supposed to be the episode's climax, she wrestles a shotgun away from one of her assailants, aims, and pulls the trigger.

Out comes confetti.

The whole thing was a hoax. Her name is revealed, as well as the fact that she and her fiancé murdered a child, the sentence for which crime is daily psychological torture. Relive the same day over and over and over again, with no memory that it has ever happened before.

Some would watch the aftermath of that reveal—the woman being driven back to her compound while those spectators from earlier curse her and damn her and spit at her—and say that's justice. They might say that, in punishing her, the legal system that exists in the world of this episode is simply operating out of procedural fidelity. Maybe the algorithm decided this, and an algorithm sees neither color nor sex, neither gender nor faith, renders us equally as numbers. But of the many things I came away from that episode holding in my chest, nowhere among them was any sense of justice.

Black Mirror places the episode somewhere in our future. An After, as it were. But the punchline here, as in so much speculative fiction, is that the After is simply our Now in jackboots, the light at the end of the tunnel, brought to you by lamps hanging up in the next portion of tunnel. If your organizing principle is freedom, maybe all you've done for yourself is fashion another cage. And a cage does not need metal bars and concrete walls to be a cage.

In early 2018, the Fort Bend Independent School District broke ground in Sugar Land, Texas, on the site of what was to be a new technical center. It was in February that the first remains were discovered. By July, archaeologists had discovered ninety-five bodies. The bodies were buried in individual wooden caskets. Initial analysis placed the youngest of the deceased at fourteen, the oldest at around seventy. Analysts deduced, early on, that the bodies showed evidence of severe malnourishment and physical stress, pointing to a history of hard labor. Prison labor.

A former prison guard, Reginald Moore, had told officials in the fall of the previous year that there might be a cemetery there. Since his term as a corrections officer in the 1980s, he had adopted as his mission excavating the land's past and serving as caretaker for the Imperial Farm Cemetery, also in Fort Bend County.

The bodies were likely buried between 1878 and 1910. Technically, none of the buried could have been slaves at the time of their deaths. Slavery had officially ended in Texas thirteen years earlier.

June 19, 1865

Union Army general Gordon Granger stands on the balcony of Galveston's Ashton Villa. Maybe there are banners commemorating the occasion. Maybe a flag hangs from somewhere. Maybe he has bathed, maybe he has not. The previous day, the general had arrived on Galveston Island with two thousand federal troops to occupy Texas on behalf of the federal government. Just over two weeks prior, on June 2, the last of the Confederate forces, the Army of the Trans-Mississippi, had formally surrendered. Maybe they hadn't believed reports of Robert E. Lee's official surrender on April 9 of that year. Maybe they thought it Union propaganda. Maybe the officers leading that corps lost the mail.

But on June 19, 1865, General Granger unfolds a piece of parchment and reads aloud from what is marked "General Order No. 3":

> The people of Texas are informed that, in accordance with a proclamation from the Executive of the United States, all slaves are free. This involves an absolute

equality of personal rights and rights of property between former masters and slaves, and the connection heretofore existing between them becomes that between employer and hired labor. The freedmen are advised to remain quietly at their present homes and work for wages. They are informed that they will not be allowed to collect at military posts and that they will not be supported in idleness either there or elsewhere.

The once-enslaved rejoiced in the streets.

The fourteen-year-old boy whose destiny is a shallow grave near the Brazos River is one year old. Born a slave before the moral border crosses him, he's suddenly freed. In thirteen years, he will be buried alongside the rest of the prison labor.

Even a cursory reading of General Order No. 3 reveals just how conditional freedom was in the postbellum Re-United States. Despite "an absolute equality of personal rights and rights of property between former masters and slaves," the freedmen would not be allowed to "collect at military posts," nor would they be "supported in idleness either there or elsewhere." Whether they served the Union or the Confederacy, they would be left with nothing but the scarred skin on their backs. There would be no government assistance, no forty acres, no mule, no "help them get back on their feet" allowance. Liberation pure and simple. A typical American blunder to mistake emancipation for justice, liberation for peace. To mistake the light up ahead for the tunnel's end and conclude that the hard work is finished.

The After that these free folk walk into is a Texas whose economy depended heavily—too heavily—on sugarcane, a Texas whose economy had depended almost entirely on free labor. So two Confederate veterans, Edward Cunningham and Littleberry Ellis, sign a contract with the state in 1878 to lease the state's prison population. Texas was not alone. The Vagrancy Act of 1866, also known as the "Act Providing for the Punishment of Vagrants," drafted and ratified by the Virginia state legislature, forced into imprisonment for a term of up to three months anyone who appeared to be unemployed or homeless. It is only one example of the type of legal regime that proliferated across the United States. So-called Black Codes declared, among other things, that if a freedman left employment without the employer's permission, he would be denied his wages. In addition, a worker could be fined one dollar for acts of disobedience or negligence or twenty-five cents per hour for every missed hour of work. In Texas, a system of apprenticeship was created, along with a host of vagrancy laws.

Cunningham and Ellis suddenly had their workers.

In many instances, men were handpicked, noted for their large build or their worker's hands or their strong backs—innocent men, targeted as they walked through the thoroughfare because they looked like good laborers, arrested and swept into the machine of convict leasing.

That year, 1878, the fourteen-year-old boy, if he is not already serving time in a cell or on a plantation, will arrive at his destination and not last the year.

Out comes confetti. The whole thing was a hoax.

By the time he died, Ralph Ellison had compiled thousands of pages of notes and drafts and pieces of drafts on what was to be his second work of long fiction, the novel that would follow his masterwork, *Invisible Man*. He never lived to see it completed. Looking at the themes it examined, perhaps unfinished is that book's most natural state. There is a dying race-baiting senator who once was maybe a small Black boy destined to be a preacher. There is a parodic exploration of filmmaking culture as an allegory for Franklinian ambition, the American ideal: reinvention. There's jazz in the prose and in the story. There's a tragicomic scene where Senator-to-be Sunraider, as a maybe Black boy, is raised out of a tiny coffin by his adopted preacher daddy during the course of a rousing sermon only to see a white lady from the congregation loudly claim him as her long-lost son. The story is ostensibly a satire, but the shapeshifting of the maybe Black preacher's son into race-baiting United States senator brings to mind more fantastical creatures, the werewolves and sprites and witches and vampires who all, in one way or another, embody our fears and hopes and lusts. The werewolf's human form is a seduction, and so is the promise, in Ellison's unfinished second novel, of whiteness. Of freedom.

Long after Ellison's death, a near-comprehensive collection of what was supposed to be this novel was released, titled

Three Days Before the Shooting. Previously, the material had been compiled, condensed, and published by his editor as a novel coming in at under four hundred pages.

Its original title was *Juneteenth*.

July 22, 2013

I arrive at the Ofer military court for the first time. It wasn't that far from the office in Ramallah. We took a service taxi to the gates, off-loaded, and got into a van that operated much like a taxi, the way a plainclothes cop is police, and we crossed the first major threshold, whereupon we passed through the first metal detector and showed our passports to the bored guard behind the glass. When we came out from beneath the shelter of that first station, we walked down an outdoor corridor to a waiting room where waited family members of those whose trials were scheduled that day, along with men and women in the process of attending their own hearings, many for parking tickets.

In May of 2013, I began work at an organization that represented and advocated on behalf of Palestinian Arabs detained in Israeli prisons. At the time, I occupied a flat in Ramallah with a classmate from law school. She was working on women's rights. I was at the Ofer military court on this hot July day with a supervisor and a few colleagues, one of whom was a student like myself but from Harvard Law School, while I was representing Columbia.

My supervisor took our passports into the main booth, and then after a wait, we went through. Shoes and belts removed, pockets emptied, we came out on the other side with our belongings. Down another corridor and into a courtyard that looked very much like the prison courtyards in the US, only this was populated with family and friends of the to-be-incarcerated. Heat blanketed everything, and people bounced in and out of the shade, waiting, joking about what they'd do if they couldn't get rid of the parking ticket. I talked career paths with this fellow intern and movies, I think, with another colleague. Inside a small shack-like building that resembled a mini airport waiting station, I practiced my Arabic script, and a fellow intern taught me some new words, and I worked on my numbers. With us at that time were the wife and the brother of one of the detainees we'd come to see, a man who worked and researched with our organization and who had been arrested and detained the previous September. We were here for his sentencing hearing.

Our colleague is being held in Trailer 4. There are four prisoners in the box here to our left. Less chaos than during hearings earlier in the day. There's one dignified hijabi woman who looks like defense counsel. New witnesses enter, and we play musical chairs to shuffle so that the men sit in an unbroken line.

The translator here has a wide, sharp face, stubbled cheeks, shiny blue eyes; he looks like so many kids I went to school with. A billy club hangs from his back pouch.

A dumpy middle-aged prosecutor charges his phone in the wall behind him.

The prisoners here are older than most of us in the audience. Much older.

One of the prisoners receives word from his wife, behind me, seated among the spectators, that his friend has recently died. "My God," he says. "Rest in peace." The expression on his face is beyond my ability to describe. Before he can fully process the news, his attention snaps back to his hearing.

The prisoners are handcuffed in pairs and led out. That's it.

It turns out the hearing for the man we had come to see has been moved to July 29, 2013, a week from today. Four hearings in five minutes.

On July 28, 2013, the night before our colleague's trial, I was in Jerusalem with yet another colleague from work. The friend she'd brought with her had on a Metallica shirt.

It took quite a bit of cajoling on my colleague's part to eventually get me to Jerusalem, and while the three of us sat on the roof of the Austrian Hospice with the sun gilding East Jerusalem, waiting expectantly for the muezzin so that we could begin eating the sweets we'd picked up in the souk, she asked why I'd waited until my last week in Palestine to come to its capital.

I thought of the Qalandiya checkpoint I'd seen numerous times and had occasionally passed through and how the very sight of all those Palestinians herded like cattle through the stations, many of them waiting in lines in a shack reminiscent of a postapocalyptic Six Flags, made my hands start shaking. I thought of how comfortable I'd gotten in Ramallah, even as this place had begun to wear on my spirit. It was familiar. More familiar than leaving.

And I thought of everywhere else I'd traveled to. For school, for work, for moral and intellectual improvement. All the other countries where voyaging was an effortless thing. On a whim, I could board a train in Paris that would spirit me to Amsterdam. Being stranded at the Kosovo-Serbia border and having to negotiate my way through Macedonia, cut a path through Bosnia, to wind up back in Croatia again, that was an adventure. Rabat to Tangier, an inspired odyssey. Purpose powered each voyage—a semester abroad, a research trip, summer language study—and each territory lives in my memory as a musical, sunlit expanse.

Here, though, freedom of movement didn't seem to exist beyond the borders of Ramallah. There were passable barriers, but the trouble of negotiating them overwhelmed me so much that it took ten weeks for me to see a city that was but twenty kilometers away. There was security behind bars. Should our imprisoned colleague eventually be released, this is what would have been waiting for him. More tunnel.

So when my friend asked me why it took me so long to get to Jerusalem after I'd been in the Territories for almost ten weeks, I shrugged and said I was scared.

The next day, our colleague went on trial. Again.

After my ten weeks in Ramallah, I would return to law school, where I would be put on the habeas corpus case of a man who had been wrongfully convicted and held in prison in my home state for over eighteen years. I would write a long and heavily researched paper on carceral philosophies fed and watered in the US and exported to El Salvador and the Occupied Territories. I would later graduate and spend a year at a job that required me to, among other things, observe minors held in solitary confinement. After that would come Rikers.

Spend enough time on the outside looking at people held in cages and you might shake your head, look for confetti under your shoes, and begin muttering to yourself, "The whole thing was a hoax."

September 15, 2018

Liberation is one of the principal themes in the myth of the United States of America. Liberation from tyranny, liberation from savagery, liberation from taxes. Hell, early Americans even liberated themselves from imported tea. What a mess they must have made on those ships docked in the Boston Harbor. Cleanup is for later. As is the burial of convicts leased out for labor. As is the release of the modern American incarcerated. And with a mostly monochrome literary lineage, American literature has largely allowed myth to morph into accepted wisdom, some facsimile of fact. The American literary establishment gave Margaret Mitchell's *Gone with the Wind* a Pulitzer Prize. And though the film *The Birth of a Nation* is largely credited with the rebirth of the Ku Klux Klan, it was adapted in part from the first two novels in Thomas Dixon's Ku Klux Klan trilogy *The Leopard's Spots: A Romance of the White Man's Burden—1865–1900* (published in 1902) and *The Clansman: A Historical Romance of the Ku Klux Klan* (published in 1905). For a patrilineage less imbrued but just as alabaster, one may start somewhere around Washington Irving or even Edgar Allan Poe and work one's way through Thoreau, Hawthorne, Whitman, Dickinson, Twain, Henry James, Edith Wharton, Faulkner, Fitzgerald, Steinbeck, Mailer, et cetera, et cetera, et cetera. American myth.

Those works that did exist to scrub away some of the varnish, like *Incidents in the Life of a Slave Girl* or *Narrative of the Life of Frederick Douglass, an American Slave*, sometimes written by those on the margins, largely concerned those on the margins. The slave narrative, that uniquely American genre of literature. In order to be taken seriously as a storyteller, in order to produce writing considered by the literati to be of merit, that is where Black writers must position themselves. Write about your people, leave the rest to us.

One of the first African American authors of science fiction was George S. Schuyler. And one of his first novels was *Black No More: Being an Account of the Strange and Wonderful Workings of Science in the Land of the Free, AD 1933–1940*. At its center is a scientific procedure. Protagonist Max Disher, after having been spurned by a white woman in a Harlem speakeasy for the simple fact of his Blackness, reads of a scientific procedure that could result in the complete bleaching of his skin. "Black-No-More" claims to be able to turn a Black man white.

The scientific procedure grows in popularity, throwing the social and economic order of the country—predicated on a strictly delineated racial hierarchy—into bedlam. NAACP leaders with their Talented Tenth aura hate it. Southern segregationists, desperate for a critical mass of Other to hate, despise it. Meanwhile, Max Disher, now Matthew Fisher, wins the white girl. The novel's hijinks involve a potential mixed-race baby, a jet plane, and mutilation at the hands of animalistic, atavistic Mississippi whites.

Would Schuyler, today, be an Afrofuturist?

"Speculative fiction that treats African-American themes and addresses African-American concerns in the context of 20th-century technoculture"—that is how Mark Bould defines Afrofuturism in "The Ships Landed Long Ago: Afrofuturism and Black SF." And over the past half decade and change, the word "Afrofuturism" has received a lot of purchase, eagerly slapped on any story in which Black people and magic (or sufficiently advanced technology) are copilots. It's another attempt to categorize and catalog, a way to trace genealogy and link Schulyer with Octavia Butler with Tananarive Due with Sheree Thomas with Samuel Delany with Andrea Hairston with Colson Whitehead with N. K. Jemisin with P. Djèlí Clark. A justification for putting them in the same cupboard, aside from the fact of their shared Blackness. That would be too gauche a reason.

But the fact of the matter is that the aforementioned authors resist sameness. With their books about time travel, galaxy hopping, climate catastrophe, zombies, broken cities with burnt skies, they are in the business of excavating myth and pulling humans out of it, same as any other bushel of writers. The fact of their Blackness does not mean they are obligated to allegorize Black death or Black anguish or Black angst (whatever those reductionist terms may mean or entail) or that the entirety of their oeuvre must stem from the primordial wounding.

If they were to address injustice and unfreedom and the paradox of progress, it would be by choice.

It is a Saturday. September 15, 2018. At a place called Roulette on Atlantic Avenue in Brooklyn. Somewhere in the emails, perhaps on the gala invite itself, there were dress code instructions, but due to a characteristic failure of foresight, I arrive at the venue wearing jeans and a black T-shirt that reads, ABOLISH ICE. My worries are assuaged by a young man in a rumpled, dark-colored button-down waiting in line just in front of me for the bar.

It's my third time at the Brooklyn Book Festival, second time as a dude who wrote a thing. And thus, my second time at the pre-festival gala. So many of the writers I've been lucky enough to have befriended or known over the previous two years are in attendance. Crystal Hana Kim, author of the

Korean War epic *If You Leave Me*; essayist and novelist Naima Coster; R. O. Kwon, author of *The Incendiaries*. In the low lighting, I'm sure there are others I would recognize if only they came affixed with name badges.

After enough time has passed, we are urged to our seats. In June of that year, it was announced that the Best of Brooklyn Award, given annually by the festival, would go to N. K. Jemisin. The previous honoree was Colson Whitehead.

In the time between when her name is called and when she makes her way to the stage to accept her award and give her speech, everyone rockets to their feet. There can't be more than a few hundred of us in that hall, but it feels like we are one thousand strong. Applause thunders. And thunders. And thunders.

The previous month, Jemisin had won her third consecutive Hugo Award for Best Novel, making history twice over as the first author to threepeat and the first to win for every novel in a series. For a trilogy of novels quite explicitly about injustice and unfreedom, into which can be read with remarkable ease Black anger and Black pain and so many of those other complex weavings of emotion that stem from having buried somewhere deep in one's genealogy that primordial wounding. In short, a series of novels that not only stars Black people, but thematically concerns itself with the business of being Black in the United States of America. A series of novels about having too little and too much power at the same time, about loving in the face of loss, about the separation of families, about containing in one calcifying body both God and woman.

UX designer and theorist Florence Okoye writes: "Afrofuturism dares to suggest that not only will black people exist in the future, but that we will be makers and shapers of it, too." She ties the Afrofuturist project to a reaching back. Far from operating from the blank-slate baseline that results from the wholesale obliteration of one's history by the triangle slave trade, she writes, "we can reach back to our past to inspire our futures." An old African proverb states, "Until the lion learns how to write, every story will glorify the hunter." And here we are, finally, having snatched the pen, the tablet, the laptop from the hunter and typed out, with our claws, the true story of the savannah. Oppression seeks to pulverize the possible, to atomize hope, to granulate not only dreams but the very act of dreaming. What control does one have over the slave, the sharecropper, the convict in a capitalistic enterprise if they can imagine another Now, if they can build, in the cathedral of their mind, an After? No, better to erase their name, indicate only their present physical features on the bill of lading, amputate their familial bonds by scattering their children onto plantations all over the country. A century later, however, rappers walk the streets of New York City with Africa pendants hanging from their necks, at work, knowingly or unknowingly, repairing American injury. Telling story the way Schuyler told story, the way Butler told story, the way

Jemisin will tell story. Afrofuturism is exhuming the bodies buried in Sugar Land and reanimating them. Afrofuturism, this imagining of Afters, pushes the laborer toward the tunnel's mouth. That warmth? The sun on your face. Prison still persists, environmental racism aggravates illness, material and professional advancement will still be thwarted, but there is nothing like the moment when a prisoner, on the first night of the 1971 Attica uprising, stares up at the sky from a D Yard crowded with other prisoners crafting a civil rights moment, and says, tears leaking down his face, that he hasn't seen the stars in twenty-two years.

I think of the Broken Earth trilogy and the word that comes to mind is "liberation." Authors from marginalized backgrounds may, with varying degrees of success, deny the more pernicious aspects of American publishing and refuse to write their marginalizations, to allegorize them even, or to reduce themselves and their demographic to suffering. What matters is the choice. Because should a Black author face the plight of Black Americans in the United States since before its inception and allegorize that, excavate from the mythmaking of Irving and Thoreau and Hemingway and Mitchell a series of humans the same color as her, the result can be a piece of writing so powerful and painful and daring that we can't look away from that most essential truth it purrs, screams, weeps, shouts, whispers into our ear: that liberation without justice is not liberation, it is simply a hoax.

May 30, 2019

On this day, a Thursday, someone dear to me begins his jail sentence. He was convicted in Connecticut for a crime he is alleged to have committed in Connecticut, and when he is released, he will, absent permission from a probation officer, have to remain in Connecticut. His sentence is for one year. He will be eligible for parole in eight months.

He is a college graduate and a veteran of the United States Air Force. He enjoys playing difficult video games, then, bafflingly, replaying them at higher and higher difficulties. He is by turns brooding and articulate, reluctant and insistent. He loves potatoes, eats irregularly, and his metabolism is so powerful that whatever food he digests seems to vanish entirely, leaving no trace in his stomach or his ass or his chest or arms of its ever having been. If we are not plagued by the same haunts, the same principalities that swing us not from happy to sad but from ecstasy to sorrow, that render life for us in nine dimensions, that set whatever's inside our rib cages on fire, if we are not whispered to by the same voices, then, at the very least, those phantasms, like the bodies hosting them, share DNA.

The afternoon of the first day of his sentence, I sit at a table in the Jacob Javits Center and, for ninety minutes, sign copies of a novel I'd written. It is difficult to say that anything other than luck put me here and put him there, but there it is.

When he is released and given his set of instructions, his list of constraints, and whatever methods they're going to use to continue monitoring him, I hope I'll be able to look at him and think of his time inside and now his time outside, his having lost a year in the prime of his life, his leaving a house of corrections for a world of ankle monitors and check-ins, to look at him at the end of all of this, the entirety of his sentence, and not say out loud, "The whole thing was a hoax."

Between the time he went in and the time he gets out, I will have published two books, the second of which is about, in part, a young man in jail. I wrote it because I think science fiction, fantastika, is one of the best tools I have to help build an After. Imagining justice. Imagining equality. Imagining peace. Cleaning up the mess American mythmaking has made of this place. I hope he is able to read this book. I hope he is able to read *Riot Baby* and know that I tried my best.

I hope he makes it to the end.

I wrote it for him.

I Have No Mouth and I Must Scream:
The Duty of the Black Writer During Times of American Unrest

1

At some point on the night of November 24, 2015, the Foodtown grocery at 148th and St. Nicholas caught fire.

In the spring of that year, I had graduated from Columbia Law School and was, that fall, living in Harlem and working as a volunteer assistant attorney general and Civil Rights Fellow with the Office of the New York State Attorney General. Twice daily, five days a week, I would pass that Foodtown grocery store, heading to and from a job where I and fewer than a dozen others were tasked with enforcing federal and local civil rights laws for the State of New York. By the time I passed that intersection on the morning after the fire, the front window was gone and inside was nothing but bitumen.

A haze hung over much of that morning. It followed me down into the Financial District, where we were headquartered at the time. Despite the luminosity outside, my office was shrouded in darkness. I'd made the mistake the night prior of watching the recently released dashcam footage of Laquan McDonald's final moments. The incident itself takes place near the end of the seven-minute clip. Much of the video is taken up with reckless driving and distorted sound. One hears, instead of a siren wailing, a dying thing, drowning. Such videos were legion back then. Social media was lousy with them. They spawned and consumed Facebook News Feeds and Twitter timelines like cancer cells. At some point, they lose their power to shock and induce only numbness, in part because the result is almost always the same: that cavernous yawning that faces the colored American public where justice or restitution or vengeance should be found. Sometimes, however, the horror leaps back out and becomes a visceral, churning thing. It scoops out insides and it renders nerve endings more sensitive, sets them afire, and it cripples the muscles that hold one up. The heart deflates, and one feels, instead of a deadening, a dying.

I joked morosely with a South Asian colleague about "calling in Black" that morning. There we stood, on our floor, saddled with our mission of enforcing the laws guaranteeing civil rights for the people of the State of New York, and Chicago had purchased so much real estate in our minds.

* * *

A year prior, on November 25, 2014, I woke up to news that the grand jury had declined to indict Darren Wilson for the murder of Michael Brown. The following week, Daniel Pantaleo's case met the same result following his murder of Eric Garner on Staten Island.

Facebook had been prompting users to share "memories" of specific days in years past, anniversaries for which you can repost particular status updates or pictures or linked pages. November 25, 2014, I'd written the following Facebook status: "I just . . . I don't know how not to be angry anymore." Nineteen likes. One comment. One share.

The weekend prior to the grocery store fire was the Harvard-Yale football game. At the Black Yale tailgate was a throng of the radiant people of color I was privileged to spend time with, some of whom I met in person for the very first time that day. The day was a reminder that joy can take corporeal form, that luminescence can be a felt thing, an inlying experience where the entire body is rendered clement. A comforter has wrapped itself around one's insides. Smiles glow. Hugs calm the chaos of warm things. Where normally one speaks, one instead sings. Dancing becomes a thing larger than oneself. We moved as a swarm, as a glorious, teeming mass bulging against the bounds of that tent, a single organism thrumming with life and love. Love of self. Love of each other. Love of the fact of our Blackness. The weekend of the Harvard-Yale football game was also notable for me because I got to spend time with a man I'd styled as a bit of an older brother.

We spoke, and when I asked about these videos of police-initiated executions and atrocity porn, I had ISIS on my mind. At what point does it become that? Atrocity porn? In the back of my mind was an image from a glossy page of *Dabiq*, the monthly online magazine once upon a time produced by ISIS. In it, a child holds a severed head aloft. Toward the end of the video of Laquan McDonald's murder, he lies still on the ground, and puffs arise from his body and from the concrete where bullets strike. Moments earlier, the first bullets had twirled him in a grotesque pirouette that preceded his collapse. To write of his death this way approaches sacrilege. There was nothing beautiful or aesthetically intelligent about the destruction of his body. There isn't a sentence in the world that can make it anything other than the abominable and heinous act it was. But the words are that to which I flee when confronted by the confusing and the hurtful and the lessening. We were both writers, this man and I. Words were how we organized the universe. So, after the Harvard-Yale weekend, this was how we talked about Laquan McDonald and Facebook and how it fucked you all the way up. Subject and verb and simile and metaphor. The murder is the severing of the head. Social media is the pike on which it is planted.

The video of journalist Steven Sotloff's beheading shows him wearing a lapel microphone. The wind would have made sound difficult to catch. The video does not show the actual act. Just the beginning, a fade to black, then the result. The camera then pans to the next hostage. It's gratuitous and primal and obscene. No message superimposed on the video can counter the exorbitant violence. The exorbitant violence is the point. Further along the spectrum, approaching its grittier gonzo incarnation, is the grainy cell phone video footage taken by jihadis. Snapchats of executions. Vines replaying mutilations. A masked jihadi holding up a severed head in one hand and throwing up a gang sign with the other. Caption: "Chillin' with my homie . . . or what's left of him."

July 7, 2016: I'm just over a month away from the end of my time as a Civil Rights Fellow with the New York Attorney General's office. I'm proud of the work I've done, assisting in investigations of employment discrimination, handling settlement negotiations with corporations that broke the law, working on campaigns to ease reentry for the formerly incarcerated. I feel as though I've played a part in progress. That morning, I log on to Facebook to see status updates about a video posted the night before. A livestream. Before I can click it open, it autoplays, and I watch Philando Castile die on camera.

Gene Demby wrote in August of 2015 about the particular psychic toll that afflicted reporters of color who had fallen upon this particular beat: Black reporters reporting Black death.

He writes:

We might do well to consider what it means that there's an emerging, highly valued professional class of black reporters at boldface publications reporting on the shortchanging of black life in this country. They're investigating police killings and segregated schools and racist housing policies and ballooning petty fines while their loved ones, or people who look like their loved ones, are out there living those stories. What it means . . . that we quite literally have skin in the game.

A version of the same condition afflicts citizens of color in general. It's still someone who looks like us who is collapsing amid the recorded mutilation of his own body.

And when you find that name-turned-hashtag, or that latest released recording of dashcam footage pop up on Facebook, joy, along with the prospect of it, dies.

And there I was, walking past that hollowed-out grocery store that November night, writing. Struggling with the possibility that this writing does nothing.

I know it is a thing that brings me joy. I feel useful doing it, even if that feeling is an illusion, smoke keeping me from seeing a difficult truth reflected back at me. Writing will not rebuild the Foodtown that went up in flames that night. It will not restock it with cereal and toilet paper and canola oil. But terror abates when I write.

* * *

Since before Ralph Ellison's *Invisible Man*, narratives by Black Americans about Black Americans have performed a sort of zoological function. In conjunction with or perhaps with utter disregard for a work's literary merits (depending on its audience), a reader might approach such a book the way they might watch a documentary. Smooth narration, sound structure. A chance to learn something new about seahorses. "A window into the condition of contemporary Black America," reads the breathless blurb or pull quote on the cover. And in that book are likely breathtaking sentences, arresting paragraphs, gorgeous scene endings depicting the worst day of a Black character's life. The sentences will sing in a story about slavery. The hunger for this sort of story exists outside the Black writer. After all, it was William Styron, descended from slave owners, who won the Pulitzer for *The Confessions of Nat Turner*. But publishing is so often a closed ecosystem, and when that hunger is in the air, that air cannot help but enter the lungs of a Black writer who walks into the room and takes a seat at the table. The white gaze is the Eye of Sauron twice. Consciously or not, you write in or through or around that hunger. And maybe you give them *Illmatic*. You give them reportage in the form of fiction. You give them drama and beatific prose and, for the non-Black audience, that transcendence that good fiction always offers. You also give them an education.

Yet to depict Blackness as existing wholly at the same grievous register is not only incorrect, it's also boring. Absent the vibrancy of Dhonielle Clayton's *The Belles*, absent the joyous kineticism of a Miles Morales at the height of his powers, absent the scope of Chimamanda Ngozi Adichie's *Americanah*, absent the cool-cat finesse of Walter Mosley's Easy Rawlins series, depictions of Blackness in American publishing—in American storytelling—would be that one style of cuisine you find yourself in the mood for on Tuesdays. We had sushi last night; how about something to do with a runaway slave? So the duty of the Black Writer then becomes "diversify depictions of Blackness." Black women in NASA's space program, Black mermaids, Black bounty hunters in toxic relationships with Black shapeshifters, Black expats, Black earth-breakers, Black girls in giant robots. Then police enter the home of twenty-six-year-old Breonna Taylor in Louisville, Kentucky, and shoot her eight times before she is pronounced dead on the scene.

Having embarked on a profession in which I face and construct pattern and motif and structure, in which threads of theme and imagery are tied just so in order to hold the tapestry together, I look at the increasingly diverse depictions of Blackness in American storytelling. And I look at the murders that, through the efforts of activists on the ground, made national news in May 2020. And I know intellectually that learning something about the lives of others is supposed to make one more tolerant. But I can't help fearing that the more non-Black people know about us—the more white people know about us—the more they have to hate.

* * *

To look at Emmett Till's face in 2020 isn't to see a boy but to see an act. A catalyst. Mamie Till knew this as early as 1955, that her son had been mutilated into a symbol. She is recalled to have said, on the decision to have an open casket at his funeral, "I wanted the world to see what they did to my baby." I'm not in the minds of every single person who retweeted or shared or reposted video of George Floyd's murder or Walter Scott's or Eric Garner's or Philando Castile's or Tamir Rice's, but I wonder how many of those people, in their rush to signal their own personal outrage and, by extension, their virtue, saw a specific and individualized human being and how many saw an act. A catalyst. The beheading performs the same function, the erasure of humanity, so that all that remains are grunts and fucking and scratching ourselves. Watching video of police-initiated executions does something to me that brings me closer to that, hits a particular pitch at which the tuning fork is activated. But to watch it is also to be reminded of the activism that attends the aftermath and the preceding, that Laquan McDonald was more than a figure in a snuff film. They all were.

Still. I had to be told that George Floyd cried for his mother as that Minneapolis police officer crushed the life out of him. I had to be told because I could not make it far enough into the video to hear it for myself.

Before long, the Foodtown stopped being a husk and became, once again, a place in which people moved and bought sustenance. A place where babies wailed while being held by their mothers, where young adults shopped for dinner ingredients, where people went about the business of being human. A teeming mass, contained beneath a tent. A single organism thrumming with life.

And something of this will be turned into a book, I remember thinking at the time, walking past the restored grocery store. A book in which a Black boy can joke and be young and be smart and be angry and aimless and have a family, and writing it will feel less like writing and more like bearing witness. And he'll have a sister—in fact, she has already been written—and she'll be capable of unimaginable things. She'll want to save him from this. And she'll be able to fly.

Across the street and a few blocks down from that Foodtown was a bodega where I would get a more-than-occasional bacon-egg-and-cheese on a roll to get me through my commute and much of the morning.

I knew that corner and that bodega would be in my book.

At some point on the night of May 29, 2020, snipers positioned themselves on rooftops throughout Dallas, Texas. That same evening, according to reports from *The Guardian*, New York state senator Zellnor Myrie and state assembly member Diana Richardson were pepper sprayed and handcuffed. Among those also chased by police during the George Floyd protest outside Brooklyn's Barclays Center was Lynn Nottage, two-time Pulitzer Prize–winning playwright. In Louisville,

Kentucky, that night, TV news correspondent Kaitlin Rust was reporting on local protests when a police officer aimed at her and her cameraperson and fired pepper bullets. In Atlanta, demonstrators set fire to a police cruiser during a protest outside the CNN building. What many news stories failed to report is that hidden in that CNN building is a police precinct.

In Dallas, a reporter for *The Dallas Morning News* asked a protester what had brought him out that night. The man began to weep. Through his tears, he said, "I write to my senators. I write to my representatives. I just don't know what to do anymore."

The media waterfalling down my Twitter timeline and flooding through Instagram Stories the last week of May 2020 evoked and still evoke a different genre of feeling from what happens when I watch someone who looks like me murdered on a screen. I watch these things like I watched Minneapolis the night prior.

In one video during that night's conflagration, you can see the city in the distance. Bent columns of smoke billow into the air. The Third Precinct has been set on fire. Just next to it, fireworks shoot into the sky.

On my back porch, I held my phone in my lap and I watched that precinct burn and I saw those fireworks light up the night sky and I thought, Good.

And something of this is in my book, I remember thinking at the time. A book in which a Black boy can hurt and get older and be smart and be sad and want to escape occupation and fail and have a family, and where having written it felt less like writing and more like bearing witness. And this boy had a sister and she would be capable of unimaginable things. She wanted to save him from this. And she was able to fly.

On Minnehaha Avenue South, bounded by Interstate 35W on the west and by the Mississippi River on the east, beneath a flower head of fireworks was a police precinct ablaze.

I knew that image. It was in my book.

2

The week of these protests began with video of a white woman in Central Park who was asked to leash a dog she had brought into an area where it wasn't permitted. She proceeded to call the police on the Black man who had admonished her to not break the rules of the space, claiming falsely that the man was threatening her. During the video, when it appears she is not getting the desired response from police dispatch, she raises the pitch of her voice, adjusts the tenor, and tweaks the decibels to communicate distress and the threat of imminent harm. *If I pretend hard enough, the police will come and remove this man for me.* And many who saw that video knew what "remove" would entail. Images of Emmett Till's mutilated corpse were not far from the cognitive surface. The week ended with a police precinct in flames. Throughout that week, people in the publishing industry reached out—editors, agents, bloggers, reviewers, fellow writers—recognizing the enormity of the tax suffered by Black Americans, the water having boiled over the lip of the pot yet again, sizzling as it hit the stove. And they offered condolences and solace. They sent me their surprise at having discovered how much the fear of white Americans governs my waking hours, and on the heels of that, they sent me their sorrow. By Friday night, it had become difficult to keep up with all the messages, to assure loved ones of my well-being, to provide links to bail funds and other apt repositories for donations, to give advice, to say something, to combat that impulse.

And therein lies the conundrum.

Protesters come down to one knee and raise their hands above their heads in Memphis, this same Memphis where Dr. Martin Luther King Jr. was shot in the face and killed, and I can't escape the double-barreled fact that I've made a burgeoning career out of words and, at the same time, have skin in this game. How responsible is it, during this period of unrest, amid the call for Black voices on the subject, to want time to be left alone, to chase joy in the hum of an Xbox?

The "See Something, Say Something" of being a Black writer in an America that has never reckoned with its Original Sin comes with the added mandate of saying something "responsible." Perhaps dusting off a platitude or urging calm or assuaging worries of division. Whitewash an MLK quote, dress it as inoffensively as possible, dab some Eau de "It's Okay" on its neck, and send it out into the world. Perhaps caution against the destruction of property. Castigate the Black "looters" while slyly avoiding mention of the fact that they live in communities less under-resourced than pillaged and built on land not found but stolen. And be sure to tut-tut confrontation with police, casting your concern as "You know how these cops are" rather than "Don't get out of line." It's about your safety, you see. Encourage the retweets and the Instagram posts about interracial solidarity. Don't worry about whether the work is being done off-screen. It's advised, also, that you not point out the hypocrisy in cheering revolution on-screen while ignoring, even vilifying it outside your window. Politics has no place in speculative fiction, you are told. Not in a novel, not in a piece of nonfiction. Why bring up race? We were talking about Rand al'Thor.

Because, you see, when you're on that stage and we get to the Q&A and that audience member raises their hand and is called on and asks their question, they're not looking for answers, they're looking for hope. And you're to give it to them. When they ask for ideas on how to be of service, you give them those too. You give and give and are afforded only a few opportunities every three or four months to tell people to stop asking and do their own homework before you're called upon to give and give and give again. To point people in the direction of organizations they can donate to, to advise them on how they can best respect the efforts of local activists and not Columbus their way into a movement, to inform them of the varied ways through which the existential threat of white supremacy makes itself manifest in your life day after day after day.

You are not permitted to watch a police precinct erupt into flames under a canopy of fireworks and whisper to yourself, "Good."

People have pointed to the earliest phase of the coronavirus pandemic as having shown us a glimpse of an alternate reality; where residents of East Hollywood can see a smogless sky; where industries that demanded people live in overpriced cities for work are now forced to reveal that work-from-home has, for quite some time, been a viable option; a reality where capital's vise grip on American society has loosened just a little bit. But the pernicious, persistent thought on the heels of that vision is the intractability of so many societal inequities. How do we know that, if this ends, we don't revert to a shade of our Old Normal? How do we know we won't return to the embrace of familiar hellions?

The pandemic has laid bare the horrors we regularly inflict—through institutional neglect and outright cruelty—on our incarcerated. It has laid bare the racialization of socioeconomic inequality in titanic and tragic fashion. And it has laid bare just how much we undervalue those we have discovered are invaluable. Our nurses, our grocery store clerks, our postal workers, our bus drivers. All of these people are suddenly "essential." (We dare not say "expendable.")

If my profession demands that I am constantly imagining alternate realities—possible futures and parallel presents—then how do I explain this pessimism? The New Deal that pulled the United States out of the Great Depression was unevenly distributed, as every future that has arrived inevitably is. Decades after the expansion of queer rights following the devastation of the AIDS epidemic, rates of homicide and neglect among queer communities of color reveal a stark divide. And looming over all of this is corporate co-optation. Who hasn't yet seen a TV advertisement or YouTube ad from a corporation with soothing music and a message that "we care"?

It feels irresponsible to be publicly pessimistic at a time like this. To look at the rates of COVID-19-related deaths among white, Black, and Latino populations in the US and see continuity with every public health crisis that has befallen this nation, even as news organizations and leaders increasingly sound the alarm. To look at how easily we cast aside concern for the elderly, chalking their deaths up to the cost of doing business, and see continuity. To look at the ways in which China's debt colonialism is further crushing the promise of a self-sustaining African infrastructure and see continuity. To look at the current societal rupture, the collapse of the house whose already weakened foundation was further diminished by post–Great Recession austerity policies, and expect continuity. To look at cops firing unprovoked into homes and ramming their vehicles into crowds and blinding journalists, to see

American police revealed for the unreformed and irreformable cartel they've long been, and expect continuity. To expect it to always be this way.

Starting points in dystopian fiction are generally post-Collapse. The zombies have been let loose, a significant chunk of the global population has already succumbed to lethal pathogens, the waters have already risen. Why does imagining the aftermath of the apocalypse seem so much like the easy part? The assumed part. If there is optimism in these stories, it lies in individual courage, individual rescue, individual salvation. What are the contours of its systemic equivalent? Systemic salvation, a society intent on rescue, can such a thing ever exist?

The night George Floyd was killed, police fired tear gas into a crowd of unarmed, nonviolent demonstrators. They did this during a pandemic borne of a respiratory virus. As I write this sentence, police are firing tear gas into a crowd of demonstrators in Oakland, California.

This is about where the hopeful platitude would go. Or at least, if I want a messier, grittier button to an essay, where some vague desire for a better future might fit. I might refer back to that earlier bit about the Harvard-Yale game, being a part of that glorious Black organism, swag-surfing under that tent, rejoicing in the beautiful, living chaos of warm things. Or maybe the rebuilt Foodtown grocery store is due a repeat appearance. Maybe a line about moral imagination that loops back around somehow to the aforementioned Duty of the Black Writer™. But the rhythm is off. And hope was not what

I felt when I wrote *Riot Baby*, when I dreamed up the girl who could fly. It is not what I feel now. I felt hope neither in witnessing the consequences Amy Cooper suffered for what she did in Central Park nor in seeing charges of third-degree murder and manslaughter brought against the officer who killed George Floyd. What happened after the snuff film of Ahmaud Arbery's murder inspires no hope. Neither do the pledges of legislators to reconsider the use of no-knock warrants by police following the shooting death of Breonna Taylor. In the face of an Aggressive Menace dripping with contempt for your humanity and wishing, when it cannot exploit you, to punish you, to terrorize and torment you, what use is hope?

My vision of fireworks returns.

Select Difficulty

Level 1. Catch Fire

It begins with a virus.

Then, after the apocalypse, you wake up in Boston.

Leafless tree branches, either pockmarked with the white of residual radiation or mere silhouetted skeletons against a sky that is always the wrong color. Fog running along war-created riverbeds to hide mutated dogs and two-headed bear-wolves and zombies that run too fast. In the towns you happen across, people trying to kill you fill the alleyways between the brick apartment buildings. Military convoys rumble down concrete streets. Armed guards, dressed in the all-black of a steroidal SWAT team or the rags of a band of marauders, swarm around concrete barricades. Storefronts are hollowed out, but occasional supplies will glow when you near them: scissors, gauze, ammunition for your .45; tin cans, the irradiated hide of an unnatural animal, ammo for your customized nine-millimeter.

Shortly after returning home from a post–law school year spent starving in New York, I'd played *The Last of Us Remastered* for the PS4. As preamble to the exercise, I played through the original *Gears of War*. I wanted postapocalypse in all its varieties.

My father had passed away over eighteen years earlier, and I was still angry. Genociding zombies with slapdash weapons across an irradiated America would help, I thought. I hoped. It was supposed to be fun.

My console hums to life.

Gaming is a break in the space-time continuum when I am hypomanic, and it is solace when I am clinically depressed. Seconds stretch and hours implode.

The worst feature of the frequent-enough promenades with what Churchill called the Black Dog isn't necessarily the listlessness or the apocalyptic thinking, the doom-mongering that occurs when contemplating the self. It's the cognitive fogging. When the disease contorts intent into a self-destructive posture, any attempt to think one's way out of self-immolation fails. Venturing outside, forcing oneself to exercise, talking it out with others, sleeping through it, overworking—all of these become imported methods of manufacturing deliverance in the hope that if one can perform wellness well enough, then the charade will become reality.

When I'm too weak to do these things, I fire up the PS4.

Starting new games always induces a small episode of vertigo. Opening tutorials that walk you through the first level allow for varying degrees of wandering. If it's a game like *Gears of War*, then you proceed straightaway with your on-the-job training. You encounter enemy Locust for the first time, learn how they move, whether they zigzag, whether they leap at you on all fours. The bloodstained ground shifts beneath you, and you thrillingly surrender stability.

The same headiness fogs the brain when one begins a game of Pogs or Monopoly, where the outcome is uncertain. Depending on one's adeptness, the quickness of one's mind, or the celerity of one's adaptive qualities, that headiness can quickly give way to clarity. Muscle memory takes over and the ego dissolves. The self vanishes, and you're swallowed by the world like after that first hit of ecstasy.

Ultimately, however, the consequences are light. You, personally, don't die. Only your avatar. The stakes are no higher than in a game of computerized chess or a game of dominoes played against family members bloated and food-drunk from the midday Thanksgiving meal.

The Last of Us terrifies.

It goes without saying that no living human being will ever grab a fungal zombie by the throat and ram a shiv into the flesh just below its jawline while it thrashes in your arms. But it is conceivable that a living human being has rifled through the drawers of an abandoned home, in search perhaps of masking tape and scissors and rubbing alcohol, a rag, and maybe an empty bottle.

Ellie, the girl you've been charged with bringing across the country in *The Last of Us*, carries within her the potential cure for the plague that started the end of the world. The storyline—grizzled, middle-aged, grief-hardened male ferries a teenage girl across the American wilderness—is simple enough, but it is merely a skeleton holding together the flesh, tendons, muscle, and organs of a brilliantly executed survival-horror game.

The game also lit a more primal light in my body, the same set of neurons fired up by gunning down aliens or enemy soldiers in a first-person shooter. Only, instead of the thrill that attends the realization of invincibility, the heart trip-hammers in my chest at the subversion of that realization: You see, there are eight Marauders fanning out to circle the car behind which I'm hiding, as well as a sniper in a house down the hill, my ultimate destination, and I only have three bullets to my name.

When your health depletes in the game, one of the only ways to get it back up is to use a med kit . . . that you fashion out of the rubbing alcohol and rag you found in that abandoned house you passed, the one whose former occupants left trails of blood on the floor and walls before dying off-screen.

In *The Last of Us*, an enemy can attack you from behind while you pummel another with that beam of wood you found on the floor. A "Clicker" need only get close enough before you lose control, it bites into your throat, and the screen smashcuts to black.

Gears of War afforded me a form of this feeling, but if the developers of that game were Balzac, the men and women who made *The Last of Us* are Flaubert.

Survival-horror destabilizes in the extreme, landscapes change, and new types of Infected appear, testing your degree of mastery. Always, you are recalibrating your actions to reassert stability. It was a small mercy when I made it to a cutscene.

What distinguishes *The Last of Us* isn't the abnormal intelligence of enemies but your avatar's own limitations. You can carry only so much in your pack. Supplies come across your path rarely, your melee weapons deteriorate with usage, then break. And while Joel, your protagonist, punches like a kangaroo, he can always be caught from behind. And he is far from bulletproof.

A common sight among gamers, no matter the game, is the button-mash. When uncertainty overwhelms and calm flies out the window and muscle memory dissolves, your fingers scramble over the controller or the keyboard, while you're hoping and praying that out of the random discordant piano-playing, that miraculously ordered series of notes will erupt that will save you from oblivion, guiding your *Mario Kart* race car back on course, defending your Sub-Zero from an oncoming combination attack, fleeing the Clickers who, at the sound of your struggle, have flocked to your position to tear you to pieces.

Game Over is the waterfall. But after a certain moment, you are powerless to stop your canoe.

My father was a child when the Biafran War began and still a child when it ended two and a half years later. According to an uncle, my father was a spy, a step away from being a child soldier. According to an aunt, the family was relatively sheltered under the philanthropy of white missionaries who had then descended upon them. It had not escaped the Western world's attention that the besieged Biafran secessionists were Christian, while the surrounding Nigerian government was Muslim—leaving aside the animism that distinguished strains of Igbo Christianity from the Nebraskan's Pentecostalism.

It is entirely possible that my father escaped all of that, that his biggest inconvenience was that school would be canceled for the war's duration.

But when he was alive, I never asked him about his past as a child during the Biafran War and its dystopian aftermath. Nor did I ever ask him about marriage, his or the possibility, someday, of mine. Or about what lay inside of us to make us so antagonistic to domestic tranquility. Whether enduring war had had anything to do with it. I wouldn't know to ask him about that until he'd been dead for over twenty years. I don't know if I have what killed him or if he had what I'll be taking to my grave. But I have his blood in me and, one way or another, I'll die as a result.

Level 2. Remain Indoors

I used to intersperse the more narrative-heavy games in my repertoire with hours of *Fight Night Champion*, largely because I'd grown so accustomed to the game that my fingers moved over the buttons on instinct. The flash that preceded a perfectly timed counterpunch was no longer anomalous. It was commonplace. I recently purchased *Tony Hawk's Pro Skater 5* because I needed a more innocuous gameplay experience than the meaty, emotional meals I'd recently consumed.

Lessening the gravity, the mortal outcomes, vicariously endured, that plagued my avatar, I could devote myself to memorized movement, a certain kinesthetic charge running through me, where my mind steps out of my body's way, much like how I feel while boxing. Or, perhaps more aptly, while playing the piano.

The plumber bouncing on the koopa's shell is a new trill, the blue hedgehog collecting rings, spinning into a ball, and crashing through enemies, an arpeggio. And even the littler personality tics that attend gameplay, the particular flavors of aplomb with which missions are completed and enemies demolished, become rivers of unthought. Moments where improvisation couples with joy, and neurons ejaculate into your synapses.

My younger brother, however, embraces games like *Dark Souls* and *Bloodborne*, hearty repasts salted with gratuitous difficulty.

We quest for the same endpoint. Faces flush with victory, we've mastered the thing. And yet I return to *Fight Night* not just for the balletic pugilism or the beauty at work in these expressions of glorious physicality pixelated on my screen. Not just for the blood or the catharsis of impact or any of the psychic rewards I get normally from watching a boxing match. But rather because doing something over and over and over again can be its own joy.

It is fun.

I spent a lot of time getting lost in *The Last of Us*. You wander, and, unlike in many other games, there is no indication of where to go when you run past the same vine-encrusted stone wall or walk through the same empty ski-resort cabin. Occasionally, there are characters you are meant to follow, or the camera will swing in a particular direction, zooming in on your destination. Often enough, however, you're meant to go where the enemy population is thickest.

It would have been much easier for this feature/bug of the game to frustrate me had not so much effort been put into the game's art design. In the postapocalyptic United States, greenery abounds. The sun sets to give you the game's own version of Manhattanhenge.

I played the remastered version on the PS4, and among the upgrades was a higher frame rate, sixty frames per second optimized for 1080p resolution. Shadows are doubled, the combat mechanics upgraded, and the motion blur that occurs when turning the camera much reduced.

You see it in the motion capture, Joel tapping the watch his daughter has just gifted him for his birthday, the hoofprints left in the snow by the buck you're tracking out west, the slowness with which bruises fade from your face, even the way the trash sits on the sidewalk.

From my very first playable moments outside, I knew this was the most beautiful game I'd ever played. By the time I'd made my way out west with my charge, the game's gorgeousness had migrated from impressive to breathtaking.

Taking my horse around, I would go through already-explored rooms and corridors of a university campus, not because I'd gotten lost but because I needed to see one last time how stunningly and bewitchingly these postlapsarian American cities had been rendered.

It happens on the faces of your characters as well. That complex morphing of features when emotions braid together and play themselves out in a twist of the lips or an arch of the eyebrow or the tilt of a head resting contemplatively against the palm of a hand.

I know precious little about game design, but I expect that no one involved in the creation and remastering of this game worked or slept normal hours. Lives may not have been destroyed in service to this cultural artifact, but marriages must have been strained, friendships ended.

All so I could shotgun a bloated, vitiated monster and watch it burst apart.

In this cutscene, I'm a child again.
 During the fall, with our jackets and scarves, the family drives to Rogers Orchard in Southington. Dad puts me on his shoulders to pick the Red Delicious and Honey Crisps that no one else can reach. Granny Smiths are in season as well. Around us, baskets filled nearly to the brim with red and green. By the time we leave, I'm too besotted with the day's haul to pay any attention to the apples that have fallen and rotted at our feet. They smell of honey, I remember somehow.

When my father died of chronic myeloid leukemia, he was thirty-nine years old. I was ten.
 The disease, as I remember it, was swift with him, far enough along when detected that it made short work of his insides, hollowing him out into unrecognizability. In the intervening years, he's appeared in my memory of him in his hospital bed as more an apparition than anything else. I watched him turn into a ghost before his casket was lowered into the ground.
 Chronic myeloid leukemia was the first cancer to be explicitly linked to a genetic abnormality. Parts of the ninth and twenty-second chromosomes switch places, or translocate. The BCR gene from chromosome 22 fuses with the ABL gene

on chromosome 9. The protein that results is continuously active, requires no trigger, and stands in the way of DNA repair, rendering the landscape fertile for further genetic abnormalities to grow. There's no determined, isolated cause.

Research on the heritability of mental illness is only slightly less inconclusive.

Genetic determinism is seductive. It is Greek in its tragedy. It is Biblical. Seen from a different angle, it is the theological paradox of free will. If God is omniscient, if predilection and proclivity are written into our genetic material, then what room is left for the individual, ungoverned by destiny?

One theory put forward to combat, or perhaps complicate, the paradox of predestination is the idea that God is somehow outside of time. What we call "tomorrow" is His "today." We have lost our yesterdays, but God has not. He does not "know" your action until you have done it, but then, the moment at which you will have done it is already His "now." The descent into metaphysics and logical fallacies is steep and swift. Genetic artistry does not claim nearly the same sort of power over us. We can battle it. We can choose to battle it.

One controversial tool, as seductive as the doctrine of genetic determinism, is the discipline of epigenetics, or the study of how the life experience of previous generations has a say in the shape of our own genes. Did your rural Swedish grandfather from Överkalix endure a failed crop season before puberty? You might enjoy a higher life expectancy as a result. Did your parents witness or endure torture in a Nazi concentration camp during World War II? You might be in line for some stress disorders. Some pregnant survivors of 9/11 are believed to have given birth to children with lower levels of cortisol.

Place a ball at the top of a hill, give it a slight push, and see how it rolls, what valley it falls into. The world intervenes to guide its course, to turn straight paths knotty, to clear away brush or erase formerly traveled trails. A breeze, an errant twig unearthed by a previous ball's passage. Spores. Famine. Civil war.

The ugliness of unexplained difficulty makes epigenetics an enchanting proposition. Environmental factors switching genes on and off and affecting how cells read genes may help us understand or explain an affliction more easily than the dice-throw of a change in a DNA sequence. The pattern-making mammal wants to connect wartime trauma to the decision of the ninth and twenty-second chromosomes to trade places. The pattern-making mammal wants famine and the thwarted ambitions of a nation that died in its infancy to explain why my father's tongue was touched with fire when he sang "Blessed Assurance" during church services.

The pattern-making mammal has figured out how to time the throwing of his grenade.

Another cutscene:

We're in a car, Mom and I, and we're headed to New York City. During the drive down from Connecticut, I ask Mom if she'd been happy, married to Dad. The look on her face tells me that she's never been asked that question, that she's never been forced to consider it. Earlier in the drive, she had tried to counsel me on manhood, had dutifully pointed out all the incredible older men who had inserted themselves into my life as resources and role models. None of them had my diseases. Perhaps only Dad did. The more Mom spoke of those bits of him she saw reflected in my brother and me, those bits she struggled to turn us away from, the more I realized how absently I'd walked into my father's being. Suddenly, I fit into the space he'd left behind, and I remembered various moments when I had become Mom's affliction, the cause of so much sadness, her impetus toward prayer. When she spoke of how effortlessly Dad could charm light into a darkened room, I chilled with recognition. I had inherited his guile. And maybe I won't ever know how much of him I've truly inherited until someone I love, someone I'm lucky enough to spend the rest of my life with, tells me. Not in words, but in a sideways, forlorn glance or a sigh or in the effort it takes to hold back a sob.

In epigenetics lies the opposite of prophecy. In epigenetics lies the promise that while I may have inherited guile and poisoned blood, those don't have to be my bequest to my child.

The people who made *The Last of Us* had given me a gift. Had lost sleep and maybe even marriages, had possibly wrecked their bodies, flooded their bloodstreams with taurine, fought through carpal tunnel. All so I could witness on my television screen a prismatic facsimile of my own blasted psyche, a post-apocalyptic cerebral landscape seen through a mirror darkly.

What is Ellie, then?

Is Ellie the invisible hand of God made flesh? Is Ellie an environmental incident speaking softly to the world's—to my—genetic material, over the course of this tour through a hallucinogenic alternate universe, injecting it with light? Changing its flesh?

The Last of Us was a game, but was it fun?

The breakthroughs in video games extend beyond the graphical. It's not enough to marvel at the increased pixel count or the growing sophistication of a controller's buttons and analog sticks. It's not enough to note how consoles will now connect you to Netflix, to YouTube, to other gamers.

Conceptually, video games have evolved. We may have arrived at a stage of postfun.

Games as a storytelling medium exist at a particular interstice. They are totems of participatory storytelling extended to the nth degree past Choose Your Own Adventure books. Forward movement arises out of the player's decisions, yet, in the interests of storytelling, there can only be one direction in which to move. And the author, the game developer, knows this. Indeed, it is written in the contract.

Breakthroughs in any realm of artistry involve breaking; indeed, it is almost half of the word. Revenge against what came before. Romanticism after classicism in the visual arts, exiling straight lines to the land of the dodo, uncaging emotion. Cubism after that. Grunge after hard rock. Flaubert after Balzac.

In the genealogy of video games, the tectonic plates shift in similarly seismic fashion.

From the era of *Donkey Kong* and *Sonic the Hedgehog*, there came *Mortal Kombat*, where the fun lay in blood-drenched victory. After that came *Call of Duty* and the naked indulgence of the military-flavored power fantasy. And here we are now with mournful shooters and narrative-intensive survival-horror games. Games like *Donkey Kong* and *Sonic* still exist. Indeed, games moving further in their direction—games like the stoner opuses *Journey* and *Flower*—exist as well. But inherent in violence is the notion of consequence, and in a game like *Call of Duty: Modern Warfare II*, what does it say that you can willingly participate in a terrorist attack on civilians in an airport? Imagining your place in the zombie apocalypse can be fun. You imagine you'd survive longer than you actually might. You figure yourself more adaptive than you may actually be. But to embed that fantasy into a sorrowful story, a narrative bent on breaking the heart, is that fun?

So I ask again, was *The Last of Us* any fun?

Cutscene:

I'm old enough to remember physical sensations, to have bottled them and set up sentinels to guard them, yet young enough to be climbing on his shoulders. My cheeks are smooth, his stubbled. And I scale his back, stick my head over his right shoulder (or is it his left?), and rub my cheek against his. He's wearing a white tank top. He shoos me away, but I cling tighter to him, and I'm smiling.

This is free, voluntary, devoid of serious consequences, not done in the normal course of father-son business; it's unproductive, yet attended by the rules of the physical universe, skin and abrasion. And the outcome is unknown. Before I press my face to his, I don't know for certain how it will feel, how much it will hurt, whether it's a small enough price to pay for this particular genre of physical closeness.

We are playing a game.

Level 3. Lune

Maybe these games indulge some fury-driven shadow self. Maybe I revel in the violence. Perhaps it's easy to see in the blasted earth of postapocalyptic America a simulacrum of my own psychic landscape. But it's destructive to automatically link violent people to violent games. Sure, there is some vent-cleaning involved, some power fantasy harmlessly engaged in. But why then do we want these games to provide us with meaningful stories as well? I can't bring myself to believe that everyone involved in the creation of these cultural artifacts is a violent person or an enabler of violence. In smashing a brick repeatedly into a fungal zombie's brain stem, maybe there's more at work than bloodthirst.

The more stories and plays I read, the more movies I watch, the more my universe is expanded. It is increasingly true with video games as well. Like books and movies, video games offer stories into which one can read one's own experiences. It is entirely possible that how you customize your character in *Fallout 4*, what clothes you dress them in or what scars or pockmarks you put on their face, says something about you. It is also entirely possible that a preference for stealth over violence in *The Last of Us* says something about you too. What it says, maybe only the gamer can ever know.

In *Gears of War*, in *The Last of Us*, the loss of family is implicated. It is catalyst. The world is gone, and it took loved ones with it. We're not trying to save the world so much as trying to restore ourselves.

The pattern-making mammal in me wants to give credence to epigenetics, believing that if a single episode of emotional havoc can trigger illness, then some similarly marked event can initiate its reversal a generation later. I want a game to tell me that. I want a game to point me to Dad.

Press any button to start.

Epilogue

The developer behind the original *Gears of War*, Cliff Bleszinski (CliffyB), was born in Boston in 1975. In an interview, he confessed that he dreamed of the house he grew up in, on a hill, "basically every other night," that *Gears* is essentially a homecoming narrative. There's one portion of *Gears* that requires you to get from the bottom of a massive hill to its top. On the way, Locust swarm. They flank you, and you scramble to find cover. Enemy fire comes from all sides as you tear and bleed and chainsaw and shoot your way to the top. A sense of invincibility gives way to panic and terror and frenzy as your orphaned hero makes his way to that house on the hill. Where, as a child, he had known a father.

Deus in Machina

Superficially, video games and piety could not be more inimical.

Not one entry in the *Gears of War* series has inclined me toward neighborly kindness. And when I invoke James 4:3 in a whispered breath at my bedside, trying to reconcile walking in His will with the little item of human agency, I'm generally not contemplating loot crates in *Breath of the Wild*. ("Ye ask, and receive not, because ye ask amiss, that ye may consume it upon your lusts.") One curses video games and God and sometimes both in the same breath, but the child generally asks God for a video game. A few years into adulthood, however, I began asking video games for God.

My first time playing *Red Dead Redemption 2*, I found myself riding through moonlit, snow-covered forest with a prisoner bound and trussed on the back of a horse, and the only sound to be heard for miles was the *swuush* of my horse's hooves in fresh snowfall. Even though I had either just done or was on my way to do a deeply bloody thing, peace had wrapped its arms around me. A delicate, paradisiacal moment. *Fight Night Champion* is nothing but pixels and unintentionally sidesplitting commentary from Teddy Atlas and Joe Tessitore, but playing the game puts me in a simulacrum of the space I occupied when I boxed IRL, where the mind gets out of the body's way and appreciation of the kinesthetic physical form, the temple of God, so to speak, becomes a balletic, heart-thumping, sweat-sheened thing. Surely, there's more at work than the incidental side step out of my own ego that attends any engagement with art or entertainment.

This has to be more than dopamine.

September 10, 2019. I remember the date because I noted it in an Instagram post. In my memory of that day, I'm in the living room of the apartment I will barely leave for at least the next two years. It's late afternoon, there's that gilding to things, to the furniture, to the TV, that has started to turn into a somewhat annoying glare. But that's how the day appears to me. I'm on the precipice of something of unimaginable weight, of unfathomable import. I could not possibly guess what was ahead of me.

September 10, 2019, I started playing *Sekiro: Shadows Die Twice*.

A little bit of background: *Sekiro: Shadows Die Twice* is a single-player action-adventure game that incorporates elements of stealth, role-playing, and, as I would come to learn, emotionally punishing boss battles.

At the end of the Sengoku period in Japan, an era of near-constant civil war from 1467 to 1615, a powerful warrior named Isshin Ashina has taken control of the land, but after two decades, it's all on the verge of collapse. A group called the Interior Ministry is closing in. During that period of civil war, a shinobi named Owl finds a young orphan on a battlefield. In the cinematic sequence that opens the game, the land hisses with smoke, columns of the stuff spiraling up into the air. The groaning of wounded soldiers has stopped. The carnage is over. But amid it kneels this adolescent boy.

Owl is a hulking figure. A Sengoku-era juggernaut. And his sword is about as long as I am tall. He stands before the boy. And in a paternal gesture familiar to almost anyone who has watched anime, read manga, or played a video game inspired by either, Owl draws his sword across the boy's cheek and makes a small, slow incision, baptizing the boy "Wolf."

My younger brother loves FromSoft games. Lately, he's taken to sending me TikToks of his *Elden Ring* gameplay. And in his gameplay, there is, as there ever has been, a whipsawing between abject despair and vertiginous confidence. When we were younger, I always wondered why he played these games. And I asked him. Because every time I would stumble upon him facing off against the Nameless King or simply trying to get through a particularly infested swamp in *Bloodborne*, he would look like he was on the verge of an aneurism.

 I wasn't and still am not, generally, that kind of gamer. The single-player, story-heavy stuff is more my speed. Give me *The Last of Us*, give me *Assassin's Creed*, *Red Dead Redemption*, *GTA*. Difficulty is, if not an afterthought, then at least a secondary concern. The storyteller, the craftsman in me, played games to figure out act breaks and character development, to take apart the Patek Philippe and see how the story ticked.

 But that September afternoon in 2019, *Sekiro* was on sale in the PS Store, and I figured, "Fuck it, why not?"

 Three weeks later, I had come to the end of one of the most difficult things I'd ever done. I say this without hyperbole, including in this list law school and writing books. Yes, *Sekiro* was more difficult than writing *Riot Baby*. (On *Goliath*, the jury's still out.)

 For the duration of the game, you play as Wolf, a taciturn shinobi who studied the blade under the tutelage of your adoptive father, Owl. You're tasked with safeguarding a boy, Kuro, the Divine Heir. The Divine Heir, whose blood promises immortality, is the key to the resurgence of the dying Ashina Clan. The boy must be protected at all costs. Enter: boss battles. Exeunt: my sanity.

 Say the words "Guardian Ape" or "Lady Butterfly" to the right person and you may see the chattiest person in your life adopt the thousand-yard stare. They may even curl into the fetal position, reduced by the memory of their trauma. I had no idea.

Again, I didn't really bang with FromSoftware games. In part because the gratuitous difficulty didn't appeal to me but also in part because the dour cast of the Dark Souls series and your character's absolute lack of vertical movement and all-around sauce just . . . no, thank you. But the monsters in the trailer for *Sekiro* had vibrancy and you had a grappling hook and this fantastical rendering of Sengoku-era Japan . . . if I was gonna finally get my brother off my back and play a FromSoft game, let it at least be the pretty one.

It was perhaps six or seven in the morning when I nailed the final deathblow on the game's last boss. I know the living room was blue with the day's beginnings. I'd been up all night. And by the time of Isshin's defeat, I was a husk of my former self. I didn't know what to do, too much a zombie to be productive or engage in the business of living but too wired for sleep. I'd been trying to beat him for three whole days.

That's how it was with many of the game's bosses. Extended sojourns into a land of ritualized humiliation more exacting than filling out FAFSA forms with Mom as a kid. I don't know that I ever cried at a boss, but I very nearly broke my controller. I sighed heavily enough to move Everest. If I'd had more hair back then, quite a bit of it might've wound up on my floor. It would be like this for hours at a time. I think I spent nearly seventeen hours straight on Lady Butterfly. The completion-addict in me couldn't ever contemplate abandoning the game, especially after getting through the first few "levels," but that meant losing entire days to the damned game. Somewhere along the way, however, I figured out why my brother did it. Why he played these infernal things. Why he threw himself at the concrete wall that was these games. Why he dashed himself onto the rocks. Why he put his hand to the stove over and over and over again.

Because one time—and all it takes is one time—magic happens and your hand doesn't burn. You don't turn into a stain on the rocks, you can fly. You don't break your shoulder against the concrete wall, you crash through it. And that heady feeling of accomplishment . . . "Accomplishment" is too small a word for what beating a FromSoft boss feels like. It's validation and exhaustion and your greatest triumph. You want to laugh and cry and scream all at the same time. You fist pump. You fall to your knees. You thank God, you curse Him. You are 150 percent human.

The strangest thing, and probably one of the biggest reasons I kept coming back for my beatings, was that I couldn't remember the last time I'd so viciously learned. I've been out of school for a minute and a half, and, either way, this was different from memorizing French verb tenses or comprehending macroeconomic concepts. This was feeling new wrinkles forming in my gray matter. I could see it too. Hours in, I would realize that I'd memorized an attack pattern. Or it would occur to me to use a new prosthetic tool in an innovative way. Or I'd somehow get the timing on a deflect just right. I would still die. I'd never felt so helpless as when I finally beat Shura Isshin's first phase, and then he opened the second phase of the boss battle with an inescapable "One Mind." But I was getting better. I could quite literally feel it. I could feel my brain changing.

Now, I'm willing to entertain the possibility that this was simply delusion or tactile hallucination, but whatever it was was a completely new gameplay experience, if not in spirit then in degree.

Victory felt right. I'd done the difficult thing, and I'd finished it, and it felt right.

Having been raised in a Biblically robust household, I noticed very early on the Puritan inclination of the whole "Git Gud" mentality. This idea that choosing the "Easy" or "Novice" difficulty was evidence of spiritual defect, and its corollary, that completing a game "the way it's meant to be played" evinced moral correctness. If its adherents weren't initially as numerous or loud re *Elden Ring*, it might be because they'd migrated to the indie darling *Sifu*. The opprobrium that Git Gud acolytes unleashed when an update allowed for an "Easy" difficulty in a game whose normal, default course is absolutely harrowing was deafening. Accessibility is weakness, and hesitation is defeat. These are the central tenets in the Church of Git Gud.

There's an asceticism to it all that, in a certain light, I would have once upon a time found admirable. I used to nurse a kink for religiously inspired deprivation. Lent wasn't something I looked to with dread; it was more the occasion for course-correction I salivated for. If I could eliminate this vice from my diet, my routine, my life for thirty or however many days, then maybe I could free myself of it completely. If I could abstain for long enough, then maybe I could relieve myself of the burden of these cravings. Of course, I could talk myself out of any self-directed program, but if I could hijack some doctrinal superstructure, I'd have the guardrails I needed in order to straighten my path, bleed my existence of chaos and disorder, bring myself closer to God. At work in the earliest incarnation of this posture were self-injurious impulses questing for a justification. And what better justification than the moral instruction that sometimes the best way to tell the right thing from the wrong thing is that the right thing is often the one that hurts more?

Forty days and forty nights in the desert stand to bring you a nourishment you may not find anywhere else. I remember when a dear friend walked me through one week of Ramadan fasting, and when I finally bit into the date at the end of my first day, beginning my inaugural iftar, I involuntarily closed my eyes and inclined my face toward Heaven. Just like in the movies.

Nothing has ever tasted as good as that date.

For a time, I took the spiritual uplift I got from these episodes of physical/psychic deprivation as indications that self-care as popularly conceptualized meant laziness and insouciance. Industriousness was self-improvement. Surely, the scraggly-bearded ascetic is some sharp-edged ideal, self-inflicted emaciation leading the self-lessened inexorably toward wisdom, stretching their finger closer and closer to that Thing Bigger Than Them.

In college, when I had a paper or presentation due, I would often run full tilt at the thing. My dorm room floor would be littered with splayed-open library books, my garbage can a graveyard of empty Red Bull cans, and I would be blanketed in a feeling of rightness. For a time, those memories thrilled me. I know now that the thrill lay in how fast I was driving the car, in the danger I was courting—not out of a sense of invincibility, but rather out of some darker incitement I could disguise as a productivity jones. But starving is not fasting, and during those times in my life when my hip bones protruded, I confess I felt much closer to stealing a loaf of bread than to purloining an hour from the day to converse with the Divine.

It was *The Power and the Glory* that finally completed my turn away from self-immolation. To call it a tremendous book would be to indulge in criminal understatement. I may not have shed a single tear while fighting the Corrupted Monk, but my eyes were quite wet when I turned the last page of that Graham Greene book. I found what I found in that book because so much of my idea of faith is caught up in palpable theology, the God that exists in the blood and dirt of our existence. I came away from it understanding finally that, as regards the bounties of my Lenten endeavors, the act should not be the focus while the goal remains in the periphery;

rather, it should be the purpose, the reflection, the healing, that stands center stage, while the act, the walk through the desert, is in service of that.

My guide through that first week of Ramadan emphasized one thing above all else. My primary concern should be my health. Health is paramount. Holy things shouldn't be done just because it hurts to do them.

As life would have it, I happened to read *The Power and the Glory* during Lent.

Since that first *Sekiro* playthrough, I've gone through the entire game three more times. The COVID-19 pandemic brought me back for that second go-round. Lockdowns and event cancellations freed up my tour schedule, so on April 3, 2020, my journal entry reads: "Started *Sekiro* again. Like a dumbass."

The game was easier that time, barely. But the high was still there. Later that year, on the one-year anniversary of beginning that whole sojourn, my brother reminded me of what I'd begun, and I noticed I was 25 percent away from my first platinum trophy. That *Sekiro* was the first game I ever Platinum'd is certainly some sort of perversion, but of what, I'm still not sure. It had, however, turned into something fun. As hearty and grisly a repast as it was, it was fun. I could finally say that with confidence.

I knew soon after *Elden Ring* dropped that I would play it at some point. I'd submitted very quickly to that fact. General Radahn's gravity magic at work.

Before that, I contented myself with watching other people's playthroughs and streams, laughing at their rage-quits and rejoicing in their victories. But while watching, I couldn't help imagining how I would tackle that particular boss. I didn't worry that knowing what was to come might ruin some of the game for me, largely because I knew that actually playing the thing would be an entirely different experience. Who among us has successfully dodged Malenia's waterfowl dance on the first try?

But I did wonder if, in the enormity of the excursion waiting for me, there would be space for an ambrosial moment or two somewhere in the Lands Between. Something like Donna from *Halt and Catch Fire* playing *Pilgrim*, the game her erstwhile colleague Cameron had made, had prided herself on, well before it all went to shit.

I think of that moment in season four, episode five a lot.

That look in Donna's eyes as she figures the game out. As she learns it. As she submits to it. As new wrinkles appear in her brain, the imprint left by celestial fingers. As she becomes more connected to Cameron than if her former friend had been standing in the room, hunched over her shoulder, guiding her through those puzzles. A whispered word, a hand on the shoulder, a reminder that she's not alone. Is that not sometimes the form that God can take?

I tried to approach *Elden Ring* not in the vesture of a Git Gud penitent but clad in more modest garments.

I've now played through the story in its entirety six times, in the process unlocking all the achievements twice. I don't know that I found God, but I did slay a few in the searching. I found us, though. I found commenters cheering on their favorite GameTuber, exclaiming that watching them beat Malenia, Blade of Miquella, was more thrilling, more satisfying than beating her themselves. I found us, smashing our keyboards, swearing at our monitors, rage-quitting, and returning. I found us defeated and, eventually, victorious. For where two or three are gathered together in my name, there am I in the midst of them.

What does James 4:9 tell us? "Be afflicted, and mourn, and weep: let your laughter be turned to mourning, and your joy to heaviness. Humble yourselves in the sight of the Lord, and he shall lift you up."

You'll Find Me in Heaven Before You Find Me in a *Call of Duty* Lobby

You started with one of the original *Super Mario Bros*. All those biped tortoises with spiked shells, all those floating ghosts, the princess. All that left-to-right that you understood intuitively because that is how language worked for you. You barely remember that Super Nintendo, though, because you asked Mom to trade it in for a Sega Genesis. Sonic had that vibe. That cool-kid, faster-than-you, low-key rude vibe. That flirting-with-danger vibe. He could get away with what you couldn't, because you could never talk to your parents the way you thought Sonic talked to his. But that blue ball he would turn into, accompanied by the sound you assumed a racecar would make, was power. He was nigh-invincible. You wouldn't beat *Sonic 3* until well into your twenties, but the first time you saw the end of *Sonic 2* was when your best friend's older sister babysat you and your siblings. Your best friend had a Sega too, so you knew it was cool. His sister's an expert at *Sonic 2*. She has motor function. Dr. Robotnik is no match for her. She even gets all the Chaos Emeralds. Never have you seen so much bling in your life. When she defeats Dr. Robotnik for the final time, you fall a little bit in love.

At your best friend's house, a video game becomes a thing that migrates to the PC. And he introduces you to *Quake* and *Doom*, and it does something to you, imbues you with a different sense of control, to believe that you're the one shotgunning these demons to death. They're already in hell, you're already in hell, so you don't know where you're sending them. It's the first time you contemplate an afterlife filled with oblivion. Oblivion and the dismembered corpses of satanic archfiends. You don't tell Mom this is what you do at his house, because every Sunday you go to church, where she makes you take notes on the sermon in a small notebook to keep you from falling asleep. But then *Mortal Kombat II* arrives.

You and your best friend uppercut each other into rivers of acid. You and your best friend uppercut each other into spiked ceilings, and as the word "FATALITY" drips on the screen, the body of the defeated slowly slips free to thud on the ground. *Mortal Kombat 3* arrives, and what seems like increased pixel quality means the imagination is liberated. He screams the soul out of your body. You scream the skin off of his. But you can't get your thumbs to move fast enough on the controller to pull off the Brutalities you look up on GameFAQs. Still, every visit to his house is occasion for hematic jubilee.

Your mom lets you rent video games from Blockbuster. You somehow even manage to buy a few. *Cyborg Justice* is too difficult. You can't figure out the right pair of legs to get across a particular chasm early in the game and you keep having to start over. *Awesome Possum* is fun, though, because you're good enough to accomplish things, even though you never see the end credits of that game. There is no "save" function. You must play all these games in one go. You must brave the clumsiness of your cousins, one of whom tripped over your Sega one weekend and froze the whole game just as you were about to get the last Chaos Emerald.

You blow on the bottom of your cartridges to get them to work.

A kid whose mom your mom knows has you over to his house because your mom's always working around school pickup time, and he has the Sega Channel, so you play *Comix Zone* and *Revenge of Shinobi* while adults you don't know argue downstairs. You turn the volume up because you've started to hear things crashing.

Ecco the Dolphin is a beautiful game and pushes you to be your most dexterous. Playing it turns you into an environmentalist.

Shaq Fu has the greatest soundtrack of all time.

Columbine happens, and you overhear old people on TV talking about how video games are a societal evil. You wish they'd shut up, because your dream job is to imagine new fatalities for the *Mortal Kombat* franchise and you never shot up a school. *Duke Nukem* isn't even that fun.

One Christmas, Mom gets you a Nintendo 64, and you're legless with joy. The first game you play on it is *Diddy Kong Racing*. Your favorite character is Pipsy because she's small and fast and her kart is easiest to handle. The game is perfect for you. *Mario 64* is too big, and you like finishing things, and you haven't met *Super Smash Bros.* yet. So racing and winning is where you locate bliss. Beating Wizpig is your greatest accomplishment, then beating him on the reverse track is your greatest accomplishment, and you unlock T.T. the Stopwatch, the clock who is the fastest, most powerful character.

The games you play on the Nintendo 64 are bloodless. Even when you spill nastily on the half-pipe in *Nagano Winter Olympics '98*, even when you land on your head trying a double backflip in *Wave Race 64*, your body is still in one piece. Mom made sure to get you two controllers, one of them a translucent purple, so that you and your brother can play games together. You don't know a life without Player 2. Player 2 is your best friend. Player 2 is your brother. Sometimes, Player 2 is both of those things at the same time.

The Nintendo 64 is your middle school console. It is the console your much richer family friend has, the family friend whose son you go to middle school with. His family takes you snowboarding. Their home is your new after-school pit stop while Mom works harder than people are supposed to. You don't know what income inequality is, but you know your friend has more games than you and a cable modem, while you only have a 56k. In about a decade and a half, his family will vote for Donald Trump as President of the United States. But that doesn't matter because he has *GoldenEye 007*.

The Nintendo 64 is your fifth-generation console, but your world changes with the sixth generation. The PS2 follows you to high school. Your cousins introduce you to *Grand Theft Auto*, and *GTA III* is a revelation. "Too big" is no longer a thing that applies to video games, because you could play *GTA III* forever and never touch boredom.

A friend who lives in the same dorm as you sophomore year of boarding school lets you play *Metal Gear Solid 2: Sons of Liberty* for the first time. You've never had to sneak around before. Limited ammo keeps you from employing your usual strategy of kicking the door down and blasting everything in sight. There are too many bad guys for that. The bosses eat your bullets for breakfast. If Olga Gurlukovich weren't so difficult to beat, you'd have a crush on her. Fortune's even harder to beat, but she has a more tragic backstory, so she still manages to capture your heart.

The PlayStation 2 introduces you to a deeper level of hardware care. Game discs are delicate things. A single scratch and the whole world is lost to you. So you wipe the bottom on your shirt, thinking it'll clear the precious plastic of dust. You look into buying cleaning fluids, but that's too much work. Still, every time you pry a disc from its case or push it back into place, your heart jumps a little.

The PlayStation 2 also has memory cards. Being able to save your game is Prometheus bringing fire to humans. You wish you'd always had this power. You can't imagine how you've lived without it, even though you've spent the decade prior doing exactly that.

But all of these games are played with people you know. Friends, family, family friends. They are all people for whom you guard deep affection, and playing the games together, watching each other play, it is yet another tendon binding your muscles together to render your friendship, your love, even more fit. Video games are a gym membership for your personal relationships.

The seventh generation is when you begin playing with strangers.

1. Standard Ending

The Xbox 360 drops the year you graduate from high school. Your brother gets one, but you're no longer home the way you used to be. Your drinking buddies at school, however, have their Nintendo 64. You turn *Super Smash Bros.* into a game called Smack Daniels. You play with five lives and only bob-ombs. Every time you die, you take a shot of Jack. Every time you kill someone by means other than a bob-omb, you take a shot. If first place gets more kills than second, third, and fourth combined, then second, third, and fourth have to each take a shot and then finish their beers. You turn into an alcoholic. You love these young men and you are certain they love you back. Your agonized screams, your victory roars, can be heard from the other end of Old Campus.

It's the only game you play in college. You don't bring any consoles with you because, even if you did, you would be too busy being a good student to indulge. You go out to parties, you meet girls, you strike out with girls, you do well on exams, you learn about film and politics and sovereign debt. You join Mock Trial. You apply for research fellowships. You join a Society. You have conversations about love and war. You meet people smarter than you in some ways and dumber than you in others. You make friends with the woman who serves you drinks, you help her clean after meetings because you used to clean office spaces with your mom to help her earn tuition for your middle school. You played football in high school and now you watch it on TV with your drinking buddies. A bunch of y'all eventually move into a suite together. You go to lectures for class, you go to lectures for fun. A bunch of really famous or once-upon-a-time-famous and important people visit campus, and you all crowd around one of the Nolan brothers or the former head of some US intelligence agency or David Milch. They're called Master's Teas. You write essays and play around with the spacing but then return it to normal because you don't want to be accused of gaming the system. But you learn there are larger systems to game when McKinsey comes to visit during your senior year, or you get invited to an "info session" with reps from Bain or Boston Consulting Group. You flirt, you fuck, you get your heart broken, you find academic subjects you love, you find people you love, you find people who love you back, you learn that love can mean an infinite number of things. Essentially, you go to college.

Unfortunately, you graduate during a recession and the only people in your class who still have job offers are those econ majors who were catnip for those consulting recruiters. So you decide to go back to school after taking a year off to lick your wounds, and when you get to law school, you're surrounded by a bunch of kids who went straight through from college, years younger than you, and for whom the worst thing in their lives is the first semester Civ Pro final.

You become beloved in law school because you don't care so much. Or because you care about different things. You're an alien like that. You take friends to the AMC Magic Johnson on Sundays to watch potential Oscar contenders, you start listening to The Weeknd. You study and you learn not to be terrified of the Socratic method. You start to hate gunners, then you start to pity them, then you stop thinking about them altogether.

Right before your second year, you do EIP, so you and too many of your classmates are crammed into the Times Square

Doubletree with your portfolios and too many copies of your resume and a keening, overwhelming desire to be liked by law firm associates and partners who really couldn't care less about the whole thing. But because you're a human being more than you are a law student, you just see it all as a chance to have a conversation with someone. You talk boxing with a partner from one firm, you talk childcare and settling down with an upper-level associate from another. You get a callback and tour offices and sit down with about four attorneys to talk about the firm, realizing halfway through that they're not interviewing you, you're interviewing them. You feel powerful because suddenly you're wanted professionally. Your CV, the people who you went to high school and college with (once friends, now connections), all of it turns you into the prettiest girl at the dance. You get an offer and you and your best law school friend celebrate by going to Little Egypt and smoking shisha for three hours. He's a big *Saints Row* fan, but you can't remember the last time you touched a video game.

You dabble in *Madden* on another friend's PS4, but after a few ass-whoopings and all too much trash talk on his end, you beg off. You hear others are playing *FIFA*. But you have a Corporations final to study for.

You work for ten weeks as a summer associate, doing almost nothing except filing one Certificate of Incorporation and shuttling paperwork back and forth on another deal, but they pay you $30,000. You hear some of your other friends at law firms got to go to yacht parties. You hear some of your other friends got cajoled into doing coke with some of the firm's associates. You hear it's a bit more debauched over there. You and your best friend enjoy your money more peacefully, more sedately, because you both are wiser. You act like you've been somewhere before.

At the end of that remunerative summer, you get an offer to work for the firm upon graduation. Your entire third year of law school doesn't matter. Just don't drop out, just pass the bar, then go on to earn $165,000 as a base salary your first year. It's understood they'll layer a bonus on top of that.

You graduate, you work eighty-hour weeks for several years before you get into the rhythm of things. You and a girl your year think each other cute. You go on dates in the same restaurants as your other lawyer friends at other law firms. You both find out you passed the bar on your first try, because of course. You get married, she gets a SoulCycle membership, you subscribe to *The New Yorker*, but neither of you reads it. You start to talk about kids. You're a well-adjusted individual living a fulfilled and fulfilling life.

You never touch a video game again.

2. Shura Ending

You get an Xbox 360 that you and your brother play on. Your consoles start to require Ethernet cables. *Halo 2* drops. You join a lobby and it's the first time since second grade that someone calls you a nigger. Your nostrils flare, blood rushes to your head, you feel the way you feel when you know you need to fight someone. Instead, someone on the other team pastes you with a grenade and you die. Your team loses. But you play again, and this time there's a bit more strategy on your end. You're learning the map. You still die and you still haven't gotten your get back, but you're getting better. You start to notch up some kills, you're closer to winning, but you fail to confirm a kill and snatch defeat from the jaws of victory. You invest in a headset so you can better communicate with your teammates.

Your grades start to slip, but it's okay because it's freshman year of college and your GPA matters less than the fact of the school you're going to. You get better at *Halo 2*. Xbox Live is a lifeline and a syringe at the same time. You won't call what it's injecting into you heroin, but you feel your insides rot. You get a little asshole-y. You twiddle your pen in class because you're thinking of that one *Halo 2* map you can't wait to learn when you get out of class. You start skipping class altogether.

Mom calls you about your grades, so you start to get it together and promise yourself you'll only play on the weekends. You beg off from parties with your friends, your group stops inviting you to things, but that doesn't matter because there's this one guy who keeps popping up on Live whenever you're on, and he carried your team once and he wasn't an asshole about it. He's good, an S-tier gamer even, but he's kind about it. He's got big senpai energy. You assume he's a he. You don't think girls play Xbox, they're too busy rejecting your advances at parties you can barely be bothered to go to anymore. Due to his tutelage, you become a surgeon with your shotgun.

You're on this new video-sharing site called YouTube and you see a trailer for this game called *Gears of War*. It's the "Mad World" trailer. The game looks gorgeous. It looks lonely. It looks sad. It looks gory. It's the first time you encounter a hero in a shooter who looks like he wishes he were this good at something else. Marcus Fenix doesn't look like he wants to be here fighting arachnids thirty times his size. He looks like he has to be here fighting arachnids thirty times his size. The trailer is grim and melancholic and ravishing. Your gun has a chainsaw on it.

You bludgeon and shoot and scramble and cut and explode your way through the five-act campaign in two days. You relate to the way Marcus silently misses his father, almost never mentions him. You don't think you're projecting that onto him. You realize there are more difficulty levels. So you do it again on the newly unlocked "Insane" difficulty. You're stuck on the first level so you move down to "Hardcore," and you pull it off. The thrill of that first run is sufficiently replicated. You're breathing in heaves, you're sweating, you feel like you just ran a marathon. You feel like you just had sex.

You get online and there is already a community waiting for you. By now, you can pull off Active Reload with your eyes closed. Even as you massacre your way through the map, you never completely forget the wonder of the roadie run, that change in perspective that lowers the camera to boot-level and speeds up the gameplay, a level of immersion you did not think possible in the chaos of a shooter.

Gears 2 and *Gears 3* are insta-buys. The campaigns are side projects because the true meat and potatoes is multiplayer. You'd be a guru, a senpai schooling the lesser players, but you're too busy being a trash-talking Gamer. This is where you're most powerful. You're a field general on the mic. You end up having to transfer to a state school because your grades are too low.

You start to hear about this new game, *Call of Duty*, but you're too good at *Gears* to leave it just yet. And you can't get enough of its mournfulness. Those damn trailers. At night, you watch them montaged together, set to "Mad World," to "Heron Blue" by Sun Kil Moon (your new favorite), the "Ashes to Ashes" and "Dust to Dust" trailers. The lights are off and the screen of your laptop glows over your face as the songs play in your headphones. You want to cry, but you don't know why. Maybe it's because, without your lobby, you feel you have nothing. Maybe it's because the songs themselves are so mellow, so downbeat, so introspective. Maybe it's because something in the tuning fork of your soul is struck by all this sorrow, all this wishing the world wasn't the way it was and yet you still have to complete your mission. At night, just before sleep, is when you're least an asshole.

Eventually, enough of your party migrates to COD that the year you graduate from college, you get *Modern Warfare II*. That game asks you if you want to do the "No Russians" mission, and you say yes, and suddenly, to maintain your cover in a terrorist organization, you participate in a mass shooting at an airport. You don't have to fire a single shot to complete the mission, but you don't know that yet. You do what you think the game is telling you to do.

You join a lobby. You get called a nigger. But this time you're good. The guy who says it is the first guy you kill. And you kill him again and again and again. You don't care what your K/D ratio is. All that matters is bullying this twelve-year-old kid from Arkansas into self-harm.

COD lobbies become the most unhinged place in your universe, and at first you're a little put off, but then your pH balance adjusts, and you and the ambient toxicity reach an equilibrium.

You start to hear about this thing called esports, and rumors proliferate of gamers in South Korea pulling down six-figure salaries. You still haven't earned enough money to upgrade your PC setup.

You glance at *League of Legends* and other games popular on the esports circuit in the hopes that you can finally get Mom off your back about getting a job. You buy Rosetta Stone Korean. But none of it holds the electric, narcotic flush of a *COD* match.

You're not the top-ranked *COD* player, but *Warzone* is where your flow state lives. For shits and giggles, you upload clips of recent trick-shot kills onto YouTube. Some of the comments retort that you're playing against bots, so you editorialize during your matches and let viewers hear the screams and curses of your opponents and upload those just so people can tell you're the real deal, YouTube's content policy be damned. You tag other gamers, gamers friend you. You get a following. You're so at home on Ranked Matches that you can almost multitask. So good you draw the attention of FaZe Clan.

You knew there were professional gamers out there, but you had no idea there was all this infrastructure. You almost miss your flight out to meet the group, and your nerves are so bad you ice the first few matches. But you know the game like you would a lover. And the other guys appreciate that.

But then you're home again because you didn't make the roster. You sit in a *COD* lobby, waiting for the match to start, waiting for someone to call you a nigger so you can not feel sad again.

3. Age of Stars Ending

You're not good at games. In fact, you die so often it's funny. It's always been this way.

You stay the hell away from ranked matches in any FPS, but there's something about multiplayer that still brings you back to certain games. The shooters never really did it for you—too much blood—so you look for games that shoot beams instead of bullets. If *Valorant* or *Fortnite* or *Apex Legends* had come out a few decades earlier, you would've been right at home. Because the point was never winning. Sure, winning was fun, but it was nothing if you weren't winning with the squad you joined every night at eight p.m. your time.

Your squad follows you off the game too. In the group chat, they coach you through breakups, they rag on the boy who broke your heart. You cradle one another when being a Black girl gamer online is just too much. While you are invisible to the world you spend so much time in, you are visible to one another. And when, a few years after college, a friend introduces you to Twitch, you're suddenly visible to more.

You're nervous. You're not good at these games, and don't people hang out on Twitch to watch people be good at games? But you discover that people are on Twitch for all sorts of reasons. To show off ways to braid hair, to cook for an audience, to comment on other YouTube videos. And to watch players be bad at video games.

You and your squad follow one another, and when you die, you're sad, but one of your squad members cackles her trademark cackle, then all of a sudden, the rest of you are doubled over with laughter. In the chat, a waterfall of "lol" and "rofl" and "omg."

You don't know who's in the chat, only their usernames, but slowly, demographics can be guessed at, and you realize that some in the chat are just like you and that you're doing a thing they wish they could do and they feel seen by you and are proud. Then you are proud.

You all figure out pretty quickly how to stem the tide of toxicity on Twitch, how to ban certain words and users, how to establish a code of conduct, and, to your surprise, your following listens. And every night, at the appointed time, they show up and cheer you on or laugh at you but always laugh with you. You realize you may be the best part of their day. GGs, family.

A sponsor reaches out about promoting its energy drink. You've seen other Twitch streamers do the product placement thing, and it irks you, the thought of polluting this pure pastime with capitalism, but money is money is money, so you make sure to take a few sips of your Bang while you game with your girls, even though it makes you too jittery and it becomes impossible to sleep when you all log off.

You're in your second year of a hard-won job in a tech start-up's marketing department when *Dark Souls* comes out. Your squad is divided on it. It's single-player, and it's apparently punishingly difficult. But it's different, and you've wanted to switch things up. So you try it while your girls watch and you don't survive the tutorial.

You all can't stop laughing.

Before long, your talk is littered with "buff" and "nerf" and "meta." You thought FromSoft games would nerf your love of gaming, but they've instead buffed your community.

By the time *DS3* drops, you're famous. You and FromSoftware are the same age.

One of your friends stealthily sets up a Twitter account that now has seventy-five thousand followers. You've climbed several tiers in the Twitch promotional ladder. Chatter with the girls is interrupted often with "Thank you [user] for the ten gifted subs" and shoutouts to specific members of the chat.

Another of your friends complains about how white streamers doing what you do are pulling seven figures annually while you all still have day jobs, and once upon a time, you wished what you were doing was a thing you could do forever. But you don't know how to tell her it's okay, because it was never about the money or the recognition. It was always just about cheering one another on when, after several dozen streams, one of you finally beat the Nameless King. It was about laughing while the victor wept openly on camera. It was about hauling her up onto your virtual shoulders, all of you on camera and in the chat celebrating this beautiful, titanic Black woman who has done the nigh-impossible thing.

A global pandemic forces all of you indoors, and the outside world becomes, even more than before, a source of danger. One of your friends loses her father to COVID and you stay off Twitch for a time in shared grief. You wish desperately that you could be with her, be with your squad, in person. Embrace the chaos of their warmth. You wish the shoulders you cried on weren't mediated by a screen. You try to game on your own, just you in your room at your computer, but the pang of loneliness is too sharp to keep you in front of that monitor for more than thirty minutes. You dare not go on Twitch, until one night you get a notification that the friend who lost her father is online, and you log on to see her tearfully talk about her heart. What COVID has done to her family, what COVID has done to her, and, though she doesn't say it outright, what COVID is doing to all of you. Her sorrow reaches through your monitor and your fingers fly on your keyboard before you can stop them, and she sees your username pop up in the chat and the smile on her tear-stained face solves every problem you've ever had. The rest of your squad joins you in the chat to uplift your sister. You are but five usernames among a thousand issuing a collective embrace. You want nothing more than for this sister of yours to know that she is loved beyond measure.

A game called *Among Us* shows up on the front page of Twitch the next time you're online, and this time you're the ringleader, corralling your squad into the most fun you all have had since before the viral pandemic that tried to shut down your lives began. You guess the Impostor, you are the Impostor, sometimes you lose. But every game feels like victory. And you yell at one another as you slip through vents or make your way through Electrical or play the detective when the whole ship's crew is gathered around the virtual conference table to figure out who's out there slicing and dicing us like rotisserie chicken. And some of your streams get uploaded onto YouTube, and it doesn't matter how many views they get, because to know that one person is seeing the joyful play-fraying of your friendships is to know that you've communicated this most essential of messages: There is still life out here being lived and being lived lovingly.

Time passes, people swarm to Twitch in unprecedented numbers, your following swells even further. And, tentatively, travel restrictions begin to lift.

You're never going to forget that stream where that squad member poured her heart out and was received. You realize you've saved one another's lives. You're still saving one another's lives.

And on Saturday, you all are flying to London to meet a collective of Black British gamer girls just like you. Someone in the chat asks if y'all will play *COD* together. There'll be enough for a full private lobby, and it should be funny, and you tell them, "You'll find me in Heaven before you find me in a *COD* lobby."

And you all laugh so hard that tears begin to pool at the corners of your eyes.

Web 1.0: Contentment

Complicated German Words Regarding Memory

1. Gemeinschaft

While in middle school, I joined an online writing workshop sponsored, at the time, by Del Rey. To this day, it is perhaps the only online writing community that has made me a better writer. The "Online Writing Workshop for Science Fiction, Fantasy, and Horror" (known, with affection, as the Zoo) wasn't a place where we envied the career milestones of others, nor was it a place of whispered rumor hissing like darts at the backs of the suspecting and unsuspecting alike. If it bore any resemblance to the "crit groups" of today, it is only because pages were exchanged and comments were made. Nowadays, one is likely to receive the note "It didn't work for me" with no further accoutrements; but back then, because of the rather ingenious minimum character limit on critiques, an extensive analysis of where your plot broke down, why your first chapter wasn't enticing enough, how often you tended to repeat your favorite words—all of that was incentivized. That online writing workshop of the late 1990s and early 2000s was where I learned about character development, where I learned about plot and pacing and magic systems, and where I began to learn that all my stories about assassins and wandering ronin roped into vengeance quests and spies and people with superpowers trying to make a home for themselves were really about me. And yet at the same time, it was a me constructed not out of demographic markers of identity, but rather out of my fascinations, out of the things I was reading that buffeted the clay of self and molded me into the writer writing what he wanted to write.

Built on a point system, where posting your own work cost points that you had to earn by reading and reviewing the work of others, the workshop turned what could have been transactional relationships into my first online friendships. There was a max word limit of 7,500 per post, and while short stories—because of both the mechanics of the platform and the vagaries of the specfic publishing industry at the time—were de rigueur, that did not impede the posting of chapters. And within this structure, what may have seemed like magic at the time but has perhaps a more pedestrian explanation:

When you and another member posted your first chapters, your exchange of critiques carried into your second chapters, then into your third chapters, and suddenly, you two were following each other through the writing and reviewing of entire novels. Thus were friendships born. Writing in speculative fiction, back then as now, requires a workaday pace, as opposed to the more languid rhythms of contemporary literary fiction. It brings to mind a profession involving hammers and sawdust, the making of cabinets or, more appropriately, the intricate craftsmanship of building a Steinway. You never had to wait long to hear the sawing of wood and the industrious whirring of drills.

We lived on that workshop the way people now live on social media; that is to say, the vast majority of our screen time, in the grand accounting of things, was spent there. If not there, we always had our LiveJournals to retreat to. But always were we at work building our pianos, watching one another grow as writers, assimilating our influences rather than shedding them, nudging one another with encouragement into the flowering of our selves, and, again with the magic, becoming better, kinder people.

A seminar in my freshman year of college, titled "Roots of the Palestine-Israel Question," introduced me to the work of Benedict Anderson, of the much-vaunted *Imagined Communities*, and Eric Hobsbawm, who, in *The Invention of Tradition*, introduced me to Nationalism, capital *N*.

Our starting point for the seminar was the dissolution of the Ottoman Empire, our eventual terminus the failure of the Oslo Accords. The year is 2006. In our second month of the seminar, the Second Intifada would be one year in the rearview. While a high school seminar had introduced me to the modern Middle East, this was the semester that walked me neck-deep into "roots and causes," of course with no hope of our feet touching the ocean floor (we weren't that hubristic), but if our professor was any good, we would leave with the taste of the Dead Sea in our mouths.

Our discussions of the precursors to nationalism at the time were freighted with terms like "script-based language" and "transcontinental religious truths," Anderson arguing that nationalism had, as its petri dish, a people who experienced time as prophetic assurance. The Second Coming, or the Twelfth Imam, depending on which quarter of Constantinople you raised your family in. But the governing edifice collapses, Western fingers draw borders in the sands of its ruins, the future is dictated by people a Mediterranean Sea away, and all that's left for those who still believe themselves capable of some degree of agency is a reaching into the past, the invention of a latticework of traditions hearkening back to an archaic, dreamtime history. All you are capable of building now is a past. The future has been taken out of your hands. Ottomans had been turned into Syrians and Palestinians and Iraqis and, as a result, had to turn themselves into Syrians and Palestinians and Iraqis.

A similar, more secular version of this happens in the Balkans with the fall of Yugoslavia and its ensanguined aftermath. So much death and joy in a single adjectival transfiguration. Croat to Croatian, Serb to Serbian, et cetera. Regional-local identity, overpowered by a panoptic ideology, is suppressed only to rise like a phoenix from the ashes after the rapid oxidation of its cage—or, perhaps more appropriately, a corybantic bull in the china shop of democratic institutions. At least, that was my jejune, necessarily incomplete view of things in the first few weeks of that seminar.

Hobsbawm, in 2007, drops *Globalisation, Democracy and Terrorism*, and because I'm a political science major carrying an odd obsession with terrorism and non-state actors and nation-formation, that book makes its way from the library into my dorm room or into some course packet for another seminar, and I'm brought face-to-almost-face with Ferdinand Tönnies and the dichotomy of *Gemeinschaft-Gesellschaft*: which translates to "community-society."

Gesellschaft is where we get that "GmbH" appended to the names of German corporate entities, *Gesellschaft mit beschränkter Haftung*, and Gemeinschaft, according to Hobsbawm, gives us identity politics, group bonds, and a castle of demographic solidarity constructed on the sands of a fiction.

It's telling that Gesellschaft is what conservatism latched on to where even a liberalistic centering of the individual can occur only in the political superstructure of authoritarianism or fascism or a Christian democratic corporatism, where the body politic functions based not on what each limb is but on what each limb does. Craftsmen, financiers, scientists, the military. A society built on stacks of contracts. Commercial contracts. Legal contracts. Political contracts. In the Gesellschaft, you are what you can do with your hands and little more.

On Instagram, you may come across a post that, in pleasant iconography, tells you that a like (here, a heart) "costs nothing," a comment (a speech bubble) "gives us motivation," a share (here, a paper plane) "introduces others to our page," and a favorite (a banner, perhaps) "helps with engagement."

Everywhere we go online, we are enmeshed in a spiderweb of contracts. Every time we're force-fed cookies, every time we do something—anything—to chase clout, every action we take, whether with a stranger or a friend, is powered by the performance of engagement. The internet is something we do with each other, against each other, for each other. And while there may be hints of a sort of class-based "solidarity"—the "media class" doing its damnedest to make *Succession* seem more popular than *The Righteous Gemstones*, Tumblr users evangelizing shipping culture to all the far-flung corners of social media—those hints are but a whisper among us mortal internet users while the owner class sits high on Mount Olympus building rockets, eviscerating cable television, and trying to turn Scarlett Johansson into an actual chatbot.

Though seductive, this notion that maybe the internet should be where we *are* rather than what we *do*, I think it was always meant to be the latter. My D&D class every time I logged on was Bard, and I think I quite liked it that way. The internet hypercharged globalization, but, in a sense, the internet also was globalization. Empires as the drivers of destiny; then nation-state governments as main characters; followed by day traders invoking the ire of the SEC and disillusioned, industrious young Arabs uploading sit-in coordinates on Twitter. A history of the internet is likely to focus on who we were, but it is more appropriately, or more accurately, a record of our labor. We were professors online, we were trolls, we were gamers, we were anime watchers, we were child carers, we were writers, but we was never kings. You need to own the internet to be one of those.

That was the promise of early internet. Whoever you were, no matter your gender identity, your disability status, your race, your religious inclination, you were, upon connecting, a person who did. A member of a Gesellschaft.

It makes sense to cast the internet as a society, loosely translated. If over three billion monthly active users occupy your digital landmass, of course you're going to have a governing body and of course your oversight board is going to have to devise rules to regulate their conduct. With each passing day, it becomes easier to look at Facebook as the world's biggest "country."

And yet I can't quite let go of that need for, that belief in, the internet as Gemeinschaft. Those traditions and values that make up what we call a community—the etiquette of being online, whether or not to teabag in a *Mortal Kombat* Kombat League match, the practice of quote tweeting a post to build on the original poster's joke rather than screenshotting it to reduce engagement, the amalgamation of doings where the affectual is all part of the social compact that comes with your digital passport—it can't all be transaction. As much as I love me a labor movement, the internet as a society riven by class divides smacks of dystopia, as though the next step were neon Techno-Orientalism and replicants. As much as we are doing, we somehow can't stop being.

But maybe I'm doing what colonial subjects did once upon a time: casting about for some imaginary identitarian foundation in the subterrane of the virtual world. "Netizen" is an imposed identity. Once upon a time, there was a border you could cross willingly, but now, the internet is more something I've tried to escape. It is panoptic. Depending on where you live on the map, it is Ottoman, or it is Communist (of a Balkan fashion). Though the surge of identity-based doing on the internet isn't the nationalism of the early to mid-twentieth century, it does feel similarly choleric. Redolent of fire and war crimes.

If the internet was this new place where we were born anew into choosing beings, why did we eventually choose to reach back into the world we had left behind? To be what we were before we were online? The answers are infinite, of course, because the question is rhetorical. This is what immigrants do when they journey from the periphery to the seat of empire. So maybe that's what we did. We weren't trading one being for another. Maybe, whenever we went online, we were simply adding on to our being. Or subtracting from it. The Balkanization (an unfortunate term) of the internet hasn't necessarily led to any sort of digital nationalism, but the toxicity seems to share its DNA. That fracturing feels like something lost. I think when I pine for the days of early internet, it may be less for what we had back then and more to cast away what we have now. But perhaps even that past is imagined. Never was there any shortage of pain online. Still.

One day, back in the mid-2000s, a friend and fellow workshopper reviewed a story I had posted perhaps a week earlier. In his review, mixed in with notes about scene progression and word choice, was the comment that I must have fallen in love recently. I had, but no one online had been told. None of my friends at school even knew. She was a girl from another high school, and she was the first to have ever said yes to me. How did he know? How could he tell? I nearly passed out when I read that comment. I knew nothing of this man aside from the work he posted, and that river ran both ways. But he knew. Somehow, that most intimate of secrets had leaked through, and he knew. I wouldn't realize the lesson that lay under that interaction until more than two decades later: When you're online, it is impossible not to bring some of your self with you. What was that experience telling me? That society and community are less dichotomy than dyad?

Either way, this was the first online community that had ever mattered to me. *Gemeinschaft und Gesellschaft.*

2. *Fingerspitzengefühl*

It was a snake oil salesman who led me to my favorite author of all time: John le Carré.

In a Borders Books & Music sometime during my pre-teen years, I happened upon, in my quest to become a published writer, a book whose title I'll paraphrase as *How to Write a Damn Good Novel*. In this day and age, the "advice" contained therein can be found for free or for the mere cost of a broadband subscription, but in our paleolithic era, an entire industrial complex existed to prey on the aspiring writer with alchemic formulas to spin your manuscript into not just a novel but a bestseller. The authors of such books never seemed to have published those bestsellers themselves, for the most part, but that rarely matters to the hungry and gullible. I snatched up that book, along with that year's edition of the *Novel and*

Short Story Writer's Market guide released annually by Writer's Digest Books.

I don't remember any of the advice the book gave, but the great gift it did bequeath was its expansive use of example scenes from older, successful books, among them Mario Puzo's *The Godfather* and *The Spy Who Came In from the Cold* by John le Carré. Tasting the morsels presented in this "guide" sent me in search of the source material and the novel that would change the entire course of my writing life.

For many of my contemporaries, "a faraway place" meant a second world modeled on the Mongolian steppe or a generation ship or a post–climate event Canada. It meant werewolves and Norse gods and dark elves, but I'd long held a different notion of the distant and imagined. As a child, I crisscrossed Connecticut with Mom and my siblings, cleaning office buildings so that Mom might pay my middle school tuition fees and perhaps have some Christmas money left over, and in this one legal office, after I'd finished taking out the trash, I would Hoover up the issues of *Travel + Leisure* waiting for me in the front lobby, my fingerprints vivid on photos of Tuscany, St. Petersburg, and Jerusalem's al-Aqsa Mosque. When the spy thriller genre found me, it was simultaneously awakening and homecoming.

The writer's workshop I was a member of at the time specialized in science fiction, fantasy, and horror, so my stories about Israeli spies, my stories about arms dealers and betrayal and the emotional costs of lying for a living had no purchase there. And yet John le Carré had made not only a career but an entire literary biome out of just those things.

For me, few books hold memories of reading experiences that linger as long or as clearly as his books do. Reading *The Little Drummer Girl* on a bus in Morocco in 2006. Poring over *A Perfect Spy* and *Our Game* and *Single & Single* while working a job in my high school's admissions office a summer or two before. *Absolute Friends* in my dorm room on the fifth floor of Durfee on Old Campus my freshman year of college. *Tinker, Tailor, Soldier, Spy* in an old Toyota Sienna in the parking lot of the Staples Copy Center where I worked after graduating from college. I don't remember when and where I read *The Constant Gardener* only because reading that book was like staring at the sun. I left blinded by the overwhelming brilliance, swallowed by the enormity of the event.

That oeuvre represented the Platonic ideal of a literature that engaged with the world. Encountering it when I did meant that I skipped past whatever worries the literary establishment might have nursed when the Berlin Wall fell, that the world's premier scrivener of spy novels, Graham Greene's heir apparent, might have run out of material. But for a man who declared of the dissolution of the Soviet Union that the right side had lost and the wrong side had won, there was never going to be any stopping.

The books were simultaneously five-course meals and bowls of Skittles for the kid majoring in political science with a concentration in political economy and international relations. And they presented a model. They told me that the stuff I was studying in the classroom was worthy of literary attention and that, if I had trouble understanding sovereign debt, then maybe the path toward comprehension lay in crafting a fictional narrative of exactly that, marrying flesh and blood to the skeleton of an academic concept.

It was a novelistic version of Marxist art theory, where the artistic object is inseparable, in its analysis, from the political and economic climates that attend its construction. These were novels about politics, sure—some of them doing double duty as commentary on the Cold War and the vagaries of Britain's class system, simultaneously—but they were also evidence that all art is political, putting paid to the notion of art for art's sake.

John le Carré had *Fingerspitzengefühl*.

He wasn't a military commander, yet he adroitly choreographed the emotional arcs of his characters, the external expressions of their internal turmoil, into the deftest and most dramatic of battles. And he wasn't a socialite, negotiating delicate, escalating social situations. But an instinct for the turnings of the world on its geopolitical axes was among his premier talents. If he himself was in his books, it was under heavy disguise. Sure, he was, once upon a time, crudely put, a spy. But that background seemed more a well of expertise from which to draw than anything else. If he found himself in

Indochina or Lebanon, it was for research, not at the behest of any secret service.

I think *Fingerspitzengefühl*, or the capacity therefor, exists in every novelist, even us essayists, for when is there ever a lack of intuition in our process? We may outline to death, breaking a book down by section, by chapter, by scene, but the piecing together of words into sentences, the dance we make of our characters, our concepts, does that not bear at least the whisper of the ineffable?

I've spent so long talking about a deceased English novelist—one of those Old White Guys, but one who, somehow, escaped canonization—because during that period when I was held in his thrall, I was the happiest I'd been as an aspiring scribe, and because there is something to be said about the distance an imagination has to travel to reach its destination, an imagination with curiosity as its engine. Curiosity in the puerile sense, curiosity of a more innocent and nonjudgmental bent. A curiosity that peers through the spyhole of memory to see a younger me picking up *The Communist Manifesto* not because I had already declared myself a socialist and was embarking on a project of personal validation, but because I was quite simply curious about what was inside.

I remember this me's apotheosis. It's 2008. I've finished *The Wire*, each box set of DVDs a Christmas present to myself, and I'm taking spring seminars on "Comparative Political Economy" and "International Political Economy." I'm writing papers titled "Strategic Interests in the Giving of Foreign

Aid as Regards the Global War on Drugs: Plan Colombia" and "Exogenous Shocks: The Political Economy of Terrorism." And the most important thing in my life is securing funding for a research trip to the Balkans to provide lived-in heft to a proposed thesis on the growth of the transnational smuggling cartels that developed during the wars of the 1990s and how they calcified into the political-criminal nexus that attended the formation of subsequent Balkan nations. At the same time, I'm writing a novel about a Kosovar Albanian arms dealer who wants to build a library, a gunrunner pursued relentlessly by a self-destructive, on-the-outs American spy. I had no idea it was the happiest I would ever be as a writer.

Where am I going with this? What does any of this have to do with the internet?

That connective tissue consists of curiosity, imagination, and punditry. A bit of the first two dies when a person passes into the realm of the latter. As the internet grew, so did we, and as the child learns, the teenager forms opinions that sometimes change but then always calcify in the adult, and as the clay hardens, the learning, the desire to learn, shrivels. I can't help feeling as though that earlier self, the John le Carré fanatic, the scribbler who didn't hesitate to write about people, to write people, who were nothing like himself, has poked through, worked his still-tender hands through the seam of self and cracked open the clay just enough to let light through. I am an inch away from lamenting that I know too much, that the knowing has caged my doing by informing my being.

The question posed at this collection's outset, whether this is a Race Book or not, is the rope fraying between the Now and the Then. "When I was a child, I spake as a child, I understood as a child, I thought as a child: but when I became a man, I put away childish things." This is supposed to be moral instruction, the episcopal arrow pointing in one direction. But I miss that child. That earlier self. The one whose knowledge of structural inequality and racism was so parochial, the one for whom the world was a place to be discovered, uncovered, and not an everlasting, omnipresent source of oppression. The one who looked at decolonization as a political process operating on the hearts of people rather than understanding it as process that formed this racialized identity I carry with me into every interaction I have with a member of the racial majority. This earlier self who delighted in things, who played with talking foxes in the Garden of Eden with no regard for that tree of the knowledge of good and evil and the strange fruit hanging from its branches.

The child becomes an adult, and suddenly, questions of "duty," of "obligation," of "should" make their way to the front of the line to become commandments on ways of being. It's that transition of the university from a place where you go to learn about new things to a place where you go to get started on your career.

There's a certain *Fingerspitzengefühl* that any Black person in an imperial or postimperial environment is, has to be, capable of. Much ink (and blood) has been spilled describing the toll taken by this constant inculcation from birth of what to do and how to be in order to survive in the White Man's World™. It is quite literally a matter of life and death; retorts that such claims risk hyperbole since *Brown v. Board of Education* and *Loving v. Virginia* were decided are met with officer-involved shootings of Black Americans and the terrifying maternal mortality rate among Black women in America. They're met with the microaggressions African migrants experience in places like Rome and Hamburg and Paris and the macroaggressions meeting those migrants daring to cross the Mediterranean with hope, in their pockets, of a better life. Or more simply, more urgently, a life. This *Fingerspitzengefühl* demands a lifetime of learning, so that our very bones must remember, the jaw working around a "sir" or a code switch, the knee creaking when an officer orders you onto the ground. *Fingerspitzengefühl* dresses like a present-day capability, but it wears the cologne of learned behavior, of memory. Knowing all of this, learning all of it, my fascination with faraway places feels like the most childish of things. How could I have believed the Balkans were worthy of my literary attention when so much work was being done, needed still to be done, on this literary front of the Black Liberation Project. Suddenly, not to write about Black people feels like the gravest dereliction of duty.

The expulsion of Adam and Eve from the Garden is most often read as an exogenous shock. A command followed. But it's not impossible to read into it a growing-up of sorts, a shouldering of duties. The Garden was only a piece, and perhaps a small piece at that, of the planet. Maybe the punishment for Adam and Eve wasn't leaving the safety and sanctity of their former home. Maybe their true punishment was learning that there was a whole world right outside their window, and that, in that world, there was work to be done.

3. *Vergangenheitsbewältigung*

Comparisons between chattel slavery, Redemption, and Jim Crow on the one hand and the crimes of the Wehrmacht on the other are definitionally incomplete. Though there's enough difference in color for a detractor to drive a semi through the holes in your argument, there's enough intuitive sense to give such comparisons a modicum of credence. Ever since the Spaniards, during their Inquisition, opened the Pandora's box, choosing to interpret *raza* as race in their persecution of the Jews, unleashing a macabre justification for persecution and the colonial enterprise, those on the business end of that pike, sword, gun barrel, billy club, or redlining policy have sought comfort and solidarity in the fact that they were not alone in their suffering. What is being done to them is, in some fashion or other, being done to others. What's being inflicted on us is not being inflicted on us alone. And the promise in that thought is that if a solution, if redress can be found over there, maybe something of the sort can be concocted over here. That's the lantern light of reparations, gilding the faces of those Black Americans trapped in the tunnel, as they quest for some analogue of what followed Germany's post-1945 denazification.

Of course, it took the combined might of world powers and subsequent occupation by Allied forces to purge Germany (albeit incompletely) of the Nazi virus, but what always fascinated me was that it was never simply a matter of trying war criminals and dismantling armies. The culture, the press, the economy (Volkswagen's reputational rehabilitation is particularly impressive; see also, Adolf Dassler of Adidas and Hitler Youth fame), judges, the whole lot, all of it is implicated in this cleansing effort. Then the Cold War starts, Germany is bisected, and in an ironic reversal of moral propriety, it's socialist East Germany that more harshly continues the denazification process, while the Western powers—notably the US, Britain, and France—pull on the reins. But when the project of facing the past moves from the more tangible efforts of removing Nazis from positions of power to the more amorphous work of soul-searching, the Black American in me is shocked by what he sees: an honest-to-God plunging of the mind into the heart. That, beyond even any reparations scheme constructed for the populations targeted in the Holocaust, there's the development of a veritable theology of repentance among Lutherans and Catholics alike. Not only are German youth taken on school trips to dismantled concentration camps, they are visited by survivors of the Holocaust, survivors invited to their schools as guest speakers. The arrow of progress takes expected detours, encounters resistance in antisemitic attacks on synagogues in West Germany and, additionally, has to contend with the atavistic fury of those kids who learned their parents and their friends' parents were Nazis, then grew up to become the Baader-Meinhof Group, bombing and kidnapping and bank-robbing their way through the 1970s. Fashions out of itself a boot with intent to grind Palestinians into dust and shuffle the remains of a people into the Mediterranean. But that initial seed, that monumental wrong that people and nations worked to right...

If it could be done then, maybe it could be done again. That's what the Black American in me whispers beneath his breath. If it could be done for them, maybe it can be done for others.

If it could be done for them, then maybe it can be done for us.

But what to do when evil is written not just into your laws, your rules and regulations, but into the very document on which your country is built?

America's Original Sin, the whip-scarred elephant in the room, provides precisely an instance of the Constitution turning against the way it spins. The Fugitive Slave Act and other legislative edicts propping up the peculiar institution weren't simply concrete prohibitions. They were symbolic declarations as well. The primordial contradiction on which was built the United States of America.

Slave and abolitionist alike—Lysander Spooner, John Brown, Frederick Douglass, and countless others whose names and faces are unknown or forgotten—asked, as many do now, what document promising a "more perfect union" would dare license chattel slavery?

Slavery and its attendant legal and moral conundrums have necessitated moral, ethical, and spiritual gymnastics for all Americans who have sought to deal with the issue that made the Constitution turn against the way it was meant to spin. For example, Supreme Court justice Joseph Story, writing the majority opinion in *Prigg v. Pennsylvania*, 41 US 539 (1842), reversed the slavecatcher Edward Prigg's conviction and held the 1788 amendment to Pennsylvania's "Act for the Gradual Abolition of Slavery," which would have freed slaves owned by people who moved to or settled in Pennsylvania, unconstitutional. At the same time, the Supreme Court allowed state legislatures to nonetheless pass laws that prohibited state officials from aiding, in any way, a slavecatcher in the course of his duty. The idea, according to apologists for the ruling, is that Story reasoned that slavecatching, a difficult enough enterprise in some cases, was only made more difficult by the non-assistance of local authorities. A perhaps more obvious benefit highlighted by Story apologists is that this ruling helped preserve the Union. Frederick Douglass, in a Brobdingnagian struggle to see morality in a document that had legitimized his captivity and would not prevent any subsequent forced return to bondage, sought a revised interpretation that rendered the Constitution incompatible with slavery. A Shadow Constitution.

These spiritual and intellectual contortions did not end with the striking of the Fugitive Slave Act. Professor Derrick Bell presents post-Reconstruction as a "nadir" for Black Americans that has persisted in testing the notion of constitutional fidelity to the present day. Bell writes of post-Reconstruction courts: "Judges were content to take sides by doing nothing. They exerted only that energy required to so narrowly construe seemingly applicable constitutional provisions and civil rights statutes, that one ponders why the Congress had labored at such length to produce laws that impressed the judiciary so little." Passive virtue turned active vice.

Post-Reconstruction in this light, and the era that saw the fruits of the labor undertaken by Civil Rights strugglers wither on the vine, reveals an America where the victories of social movements are hollowed things, such that when you knock on them to test their strength, you hear only the emptiness ringing inside. Voter suppression laws, produced in the laboratories of state legislatures, further evince the insubstantiality of the promise of inclusion that came with the abolition of slavery.

Professor Dorothy Roberts states that the fidelity of America's Black population to the Constitution is born of a desire for equal citizenship, for a shot at participation in the American political experiment. This idea, according to the theorist John Hart Ely, is that constitutional provisions should be read not as efforts to establish substantive rights but as safeguards against the infringement of procedural rights, infringements upon the right to participate in popular self-government. Having one's vote counted, having a say in what guardrails the country lays around your life. It is the representative ingredient in our democratic soup that is the most important—not just a spice added for flavor, but the principle out of which the whole project is made.

But what is all of this theorizing in the face of the reality that the Old Testament was not written for the Gentiles?

Vergangenheitsbewältigung, this idea of coming to terms with one's past, the collective's attempt to contend with the horrors it committed, is not entirely absent from American history and culture. Slave narratives, aided and abetted by white abolitionists, are the voice of the oppressed, and even those Garrisonians out there, though they shared a skin tone with the slave driver, never held the state's power in their hands. In *Vergangenheitsbewältigung*, there is a very specific "we" at work, as in "we" did this. And the closest I can get to that "we" is in the work of William Faulkner.

Perhaps the most morally daring and exacting of white American authors, he's the only guy I've read who understood and could articulate white madness. He knew that the South's victory of narrative in the ruins of the Civil War—that recasting of the conflict as a noble struggle between brothers, the South convincing generation after generation that it was some Edenic landscape destroyed by foreign aggressors and not a cauldron boiling millions of people in every horror imaginable—was more window dressing than Iron Curtain. Faulkner knew that there's a very specific sort of derangement that afflicts those who live in denial of the titanic evil they committed and that was committed in their name. The Compsons were driven mad, were driven to decay and downfall, because they were totems of an American South whose necrotic core had subsumed all its limbs. The house was destined to fall. The Compsons could not have saved themselves, but the lesson in the parable of their collapse is that if there had not been a larger societal reckoning, if perhaps there had not been a longer occupation by an enemy army forcing the hand of the evildoers into purging their ranks, an army that pried apart their eyelids, *Clockwork Orange*-style, and pressed their faces to their own diabolism, then all that would be left on the charred, smoking ground of their conscience would be Dilsey. But Faulkner is anomalous. He's praised for his use of stream of consciousness, the cognitive strain his narratives evoke, the Biblical diction, but rarely have I seen him feted as a writer excavating the villainy of whiteness. Instead, it's the tyrannized who must bend their backs plowing that field.

* * *

My characters have walked through their worlds wounded and wonderstruck, failed and failing, trying and triumphant, defined almost categorically by the color of their skin. In *Riot Baby*, Ella Jackson styles herself as the architect of a revenge fantasy, an answer to the question "What if God were a Black woman?" In *Goliath*, Lincoln, sharing a family name with his literary predecessor, struggles to know himself, to care for himself, in a world destroyed by the twin catastrophes of climate change and nuclear fallout. How difficult it is to be Black in the United States, how difficult it has been and will be, has been one of the signal preoccupations of my literary life. And though I've been fortunate enough to have written, for the most part, what I've wanted to write about, I bristle. Suspicion sneaks into the back of my brain that I've somehow painted myself as that once most ubiquitous of species, the Race Writer. The shawl of speculative fiction draped over my shoulders provides some buffer, but I cannot help but wonder if I've somehow found myself in a cage of my own making.

In his essay "How 'Bigger' Was Born," Richard Wright traces the genealogy of his *Native Son* protagonist to five different prototypes, found both in the Jim Crow South and north of the Mason-Dixon. One was a tyrant, bullying Wright and his childhood playmates. The next Bigger Thomas, "Bigger No. 2," was a seventeen-year-old, who directed his coiled wrath at the whites who ruled the South. He would refuse to pay rent to his white landlords, he would buy things on credit and never pay, and he would tell Wright and others like him that "we were fools not to get what we wanted while we were alive in this world." "Bigger No. 3" was the daredevil who wouldn't pay for his movie tickets, ultimately shot fatally in the back by a white police officer. "Bigger No. 4" laughed in the face of the legal strictures of the Jim Crow South, thrilling at every opportunity to thwart or violate its taboos. He would find his end in an asylum for the insane. Finally, "Bigger No. 5," like Bigger No. 4, would ride in Jim Crow streetcars, sitting wherever he pleased. When confronted by a conductor, he would brandish a knife. These Biggers all broke unjust laws and rejoiced in the act, knowing they'd run up their bill, and they would eventually have to reckon with being "shot, hanged, maimed, lynched, and generally hounded until they were either dead or their spirits broken."

In Wright's explanation of Bigger Thomas, his origin, his interiority, I see reflections of my own characters. And I see in my own literary imaginings the limitations Baldwin elaborated on in his critiques of *Native Son* in the essays "Many Thousands Gone" and "Everybody's Protest Novel." Though I have pride in every piece of my writing that's found an audience in the public, I lament that so much of it exists at the same dolorous register. It all feels necessary and good, but is that all there is?

A dear friend of mine from college is an amateur photographer, and we talked not long ago about the fallacy of this idea of artistic duty. About how "should" is a word that "should" be banished from the artist's dictionary. There is no obligation on the part of the artist but to their own prerogatives. He takes pictures of what he wants to photograph, I write about what I want to write about. And yet over my shoulder hovers the seraph sibilating into my ear about bearing witness. I can disguise it as a cosmic recentering, making the periphery into the metropole, the seat of a more vibrant, more just, more colorful imperial power, but under the entertainment, the accoutrements bearing my own personal touch, is a balancing of the ledger. The novel a cry to the heavens that what was done to me matters as much as what was done to you. I matter as much as you.

This isn't an anxiety aimed at novels by Black folk, about Black folk, wherein their victimization (minor and major, past and present and future) is the sun around which the novel's elements revolve. This is only to wonder at a counterfactual: In an America where treasonous Confederate generals were hanged, where Thomas Dixon never wrote or was able to write *The Clansman*, where D. W. Griffith never adapted that now-nonexistent novel into *The Birth of a Nation*; in an America where redlining never existed, where integrated communities were made de facto because Jim Crow was never de jure; in an America where postbellum school children are taken on field trips to the plantations of their fathers and grandfathers and great-grandfathers, where Supreme Court justices who shared racial sympathies with the Confederacy were purged from the court, where Madison Grant was never able to write

The Passing of the Great Race, where the level of a community's distress is not dependent on its racial makeup, where narcotic epidemics are not racially stratified in their targeting; in an America where the reunified state engaged meaningfully in *Vergangenheitsbewältigung*, would we still feel obligated to tell the stories we're telling? Would I still feel that to be my duty? What would the angel be whispering into my ear, what subject would she tell me to target with my novelistic energies? What would I get to write?

I wonder if there is another mode of *Vergangenheitsbewältigung*. One that is less commemoration and more celebration. This other sense doesn't entirely denude the German word of its reparative connotations. But it instead foregrounds the joy of those former victims. That is where the righting of the wrong is located.

March 6, 1957, Kwame Nkrumah stands alongside other members of government, all of them adorned for the occasion in agbadas, dashikis, the kente that for centuries was reserved for Asante and Ewe royalty but here is twisted tight around the neck of Empire as Ghana declares independence. Photos exist, as do videos, of the First World Festival of Negro Arts, held in 1966, photos perhaps of Duke Ellington and Josephine Baker and somewhere in there Aimé Césaire, the three of them among the joyous, beauteous twenty-five thousand gathered from all over the Continent and the diaspora to celebrate the color of their skin and the galaxies that exist beneath it. Algiers in '69, Zaire in '74, Lagos in '77. These sometimes months-long arts festivals, supernovas of culture in this artistic African renaissance. Are there any analogues, any comparisons, that could do justice to what must have been in the air in those places? If you wedded Woodstock and the Venice Film Festival, would it come close?

There's a taste of that energy in every Afrofuturist and Africanfuturist artifact. Imaginings that, of course, don't cast colonialism, the primordial woundings, out of memory but that tell us it is not the whole memory. It is not the whole past. We are not beautiful because we survived this. We are not beautiful in spite of this. We are beautiful, just because.

Poetry is not policy, but these books . . . these books by Black folk, about Black folk, feel insurgent. Guerilla warfare via byline.

There can be joy in the performing of a duty. It's not a given, but, as Dennis Lehane wrote in *The Given Day*, "Craftsmanship is just a fancy word for when labor meets love."

There's a metaphor for the internet buried somewhere in all that.

4. *Erinnerungsvermögen*

Before, an essay was an easy thing to write. The structure of it, the leitmotifs, the subject matter, it all came as a person fully formed so that its birthing was a purely joyful process.

It wasn't just the absence of pain, it was the profusion of its opposite. It was ecstasy. But, periodically, while writing this essay, dread burdens the shoulders. Sentence shapes twist into something more colloquial so that the wall between how I talk and how I write is breached; the levees broken; my process flooded; my ability, my attempts at lyrical felicity, dying. And it is an irony among ironies that, simply by having experienced the internet and social media when and how I did, I have been given a foretaste of what awaits me in old age. That slipperiness of thought, that occasional incoherence, the dissolving of the carefully constructed and maintained partitions between selves. The impetuousness, the irritability, the shortsightedness.

I can feel my attention slipping. The ability to hold on to a thought . . . the grip weakens. My curiosity pinballs between trees in a virtual forest of YouTube playlists. Where once I could hold the ghost of a whole paragraph in my head, it's now the tweet that appears to me in crystalline clarity. And the greatest fear of all: the notion that the internet has demented me. What promised so much, what promised me the world, has enfeebled me. The allure of knowing so much has revealed itself as the reality of knowing so little—not only that, but knowing less than I did before. It is as though my second-strongest muscle is atrophying, and I can witness it happening but am somehow powerless to stop it, knowing that the point of no return—the point at which neuroplasticity ends, the point at which the concrete hardens—is fast approaching if not already here. Wrinkles are disappearing from my brain, and I want to blame Twitter.

I've not had the app itself on my phone for a number of years, but that doesn't mean the URL isn't already in a browser tab somewhere, accessible in an instant from my phone or my laptop. And more often than not, I don't check my timeline for anything of substance. I want, less and less, to know what people think about a thing. I go because of the hit. Although, to compare checking Twitter to any sort of narcotic high is to indulge in terminological deceit. Twitter on its best day never felt as good as cocaine. Still, I open the website and close it in an instant only to open it again, having already forgotten what I'd just seen. Or having forgotten that whatever it was I was looking for wasn't there. Wasn't going to be there. It's a habit. It's a morning cigarette with all of the harshness and none of the delicious vertigo. It doesn't work anymore.

But it felt like I was learning so much.

I worry that the price I will pay is greater than I could have imagined. That I've mortgaged my brain to the internet to feel good about a thing. Which feels like the height of waste. So much incredible stuff on this information superhighway, and here I am, leaning against a pillar under an overpass, getting high.

Has the internet changed my emotional vocabulary? I want to say yes. There's a particular pang of longing that attends wanting to return to a TikTok you scrolled past at two thirty in the morning that has, because of something that has happened to you later that day, grown another layer of funny or meaningfulness. Does that contain the same DNA as wanting to write your friend in London about a funny incident you witnessed on a cobblestoned street in colonial-era Northampton, Massachusetts? Maybe, but what antebellum corollary is there for "I want Lady Dimitrescu to step on my neck"? There's gotta be a German word for that.

What has the internet done for my emotions? To them? It is odd. There is this grand, ever-present opportunity to commune with others, and yet I have never seen so many around me so alienated. We know too much about too many of us, and yet not even close to enough. Twitter becoming the private company it has become prompted a mass user exodus, many searching for another place where they could preserve, re-create, curate their community. Fleeing this conflagrating simulacrum of the town square for something more akin to Westfarms Mall, where we could hang out after school and shop at Hollister and flirt with members of other friend groups who went to the school across town. Where we could gush over the new Linkin Park album and laugh too loudly and eat Sbarro.

While others flock to Mastodon or Hive or Bluesky and while, somehow, my follower account on TikTok rises and rises, I've found that the only thing I want is my life back.

* * *

Erinnerungsvermögen translates loosely to "powers of recall," and, for some reason, the thought of losing that feels more tactile, more specific, than memory loss. It's pain in your mental joint-age, the creaking of a neural knee, and the fear that staring at a screen for most of my waking hours has done more than worsen my eyesight. That was the bargain, though. Nothing is ever free. And if I was going to have my experience on this planet expanded and enriched and ensorcelled this capaciously, this horrifically, this magnificently, there was always going to be a price. It must have all been in service of something, right? A part of me, a growing part, has to believe that all this time spent here, watching YouTube playthroughs of *Resident Evil 2* and listening to metal covers of Britney Spears's "Toxic," reading long tweet threads from epidemiologists during a global pandemic and long-form movie reviews from Wesley Morris on *Grantland* (RIP), all that time interfacing with the cryptic, sometimes helpful, often trolling messages of previous players in *Elden Ring*, all that time on freaking JSTOR, it had to have made me a better writer. Right? I need to believe that it all doesn't just boil down to "I survived the internet and all I got was this T-shirt. And by 'T-shirt,' I mean cognitive decline." We both grew up, the internet and I, and now we're growing old. Senility was inevitable.

But it gave me so much. You gave me so much. My worry is that, all too soon, I'll have lost the capacity to appreciate it.

Maybe the specter of exactly this loss is what haunts the verbally abusive player in your *Call of Duty* lobby, or that type of player in Kombat League that, win or lose, always has a demographic to denigrate. The devil on your shoulder prompting you to reply automatically with irony and "shade," unzip your pants and let your superiority complex hang out, before any impulse toward earnestness can gain purchase. Maybe it's collective cognitive decline that has made the internet a worse place. My kingdom for a government-mandated hour of touching grass.

Who on this dying Earth am I kidding? The internet didn't make us this way. You gotta flip that around.

I don't know that we ever get the old internet back or that it can ever be re-created with any level of fidelity. Whatever gets built on it or in its gutted carapace will never have such unique purchase over the things we desire. We can always find those elsewhere. The only thing it could promise is that it won't have what we're running from already. And that's not what the internet was in the beginning. If it turned into shelter, it was by accident, not necessarily by intention. We were running to, not running from. Oddly enough, the internet as refuge makes more and more sense when you consider that what's chasing us might be social media. No matter where I go, there's that row of share icons, and I can hear Mr. X's bootstomps getting closer and closer from somewhere in the zombie-ridden house.

Then again, what use would I have for the old internet? This new one lets me text across continents and download games directly to my consoles. It lets me order record players and have them delivered with record speed. It lets me listen to more music than I'm capable of imagining. Maybe an eventual thermodynamic equilibrium of the soul sometime in the far future is a small price to pay for these conveniences.

In *Neon Genesis Evangelion,* the Human Instrumentality Project is a sort of jump-started evolutionary process wherein human souls are merged together for the purpose of defeating the double-barreled plague of loneliness and alienation that has afflicted humanity since our progenitors' exodus from the Garden. In one iteration of the anime franchise, we literally pop and turn into orange fluid that sluices into one massive puddle.

If the Grand Directive of the internet was to bring us together, what greater irony could there be than the idea that it is doing its job far too well? Bringing us so close together that we turn into one another. Not me tweeting in all lowercase again! In the anime, the process is a bit quicker and a lot less painful.

5. *Sehnsucht*

I know, as an adult, that part of why the 1990s seemed like such a halcyon time, a brighter time, a less complicated time, is that my own life in that decade was quite halcyon, bright, and lacking in complication. Though the Bronco chase and the

Oklahoma City bombing lurk in the background, my memory of that period is a jumble of *X-Men: The Animated Series*, my crush on a girl in a white dress who I saw on the first day of third grade, the swing set in our backyard, street hockey with my cousins in our driveway in the summer, and the fact that our postindustrial factory town hadn't yet shown us all its rust. Everything seemed bigger, too, more scopic, and simultaneously cozier. Appliances lasted longer, things took longer to break. Sure, mass financialization had taken hold in the United States, the dot-com bubble and all that jazz, but for the millennial, the 1990s are a Time Before the collapse of our faith in grand institutions. We're not quite yet a shareholder-run society. Enron hasn't happened; we're a decade or so away from our ten-year revenge epic against a Saudi terrorist, an epic that obliterated the lives and livelihoods of millions upon millions of people across at least two countries; and our banks are still humming along. While New Orleans is below sea level, it will be another decade and a half before the city itself is underwater.

That feeling of cozy is how I also look at the early internet, once it burst out of its DARPA box and screeched through our 56k modems to arrive on our convex personal computer monitors. It's an almost universally held sentiment that the internet was a kinder place back then. It was new, and not in the way of some sharp-bladed, exclusionary cool. It was new and simultaneously welcoming. Though internet speed showed the socioeconomic cracks in the egalitarian façade, the internet didn't quite seem like a place where you could go to hate or hate on others.

It wasn't all *Teletubbies*; I mean, there was always plenty of hentai content, but the very reason we have such advanced file-sharing capabilities now is the dissemination and monetization of porn. If we look hard enough, we'll find erotic intention behind almost every technological innovation.

But the online space I remember in the 1990s, going into the 2000s, was a place of rainbow-hued Angelfire and Geo-Cities webpages. We would teach ourselves HTML just so that we could embed gifs in our *Dragon Ball Z* tribute pages. Yahoo! messageboards were where you could go for a steady supply of *Gundam Wing* yaoi. And GameFAQs could help you through whatever level of *Sonic 1, 2, 3,* or *Sonic & Knuckles* that you were struggling with. This was, of course, for those of us who couldn't afford a *Game Informer* subscription.

AIM away messages were their own artform. (Already, with the selection of a particular snatch of song lyric, we're beginning the age of online personal branding.) But back then, it was innocuous and flirty, and the "please pay attention to me" of it all didn't sound all that keening or desperate or vicious. It didn't have threat behind it. It felt much more uwu, so to speak, because so little of our lives were lived on the internet.

My early internet life happened mostly offline. I would look at snowboarding videos set to Korn or Limp Bizkit, maybe take a peek at Napster, but *Super Smash Bros.* and *GoldenEye 007* were always played in the company of warm-blooded individuals close enough that I could smell their breath. There was the prospect of very real injury if I or any of us threw a controller. And the snowboarding videos, well, that was because I and my friends from school would go snowboarding in real life.

I remember this one morning on Mount Ascutney. I must be twelve or thirteen, and I'm carving through fresh powder on a Black Diamond. It must have snowed the night before because that stretch of mountain trail is untouched. I'm the first one there. And I'm carving, drawing my many-curved S's in that giving white and leaning forward so much on those turns that I can run my glove along the ground. That swish of snow parting in my wake is the only sound in my ears, and, to this day, it is the most connected I've ever felt with the outside world.

I recognize that I'm speaking to a very, very specific experience of the early internet. But I've been trying to figure out why I long for that version, that vision, as much as I do. I knew less about the strangers I interacted with then than I know about the strangers I interact with now. And even back then, I was aware of the capacity of people to lie, to disguise, to self-invent. It may not necessarily be a matter of feature so much as a matter of function. The internet wasn't everywhere. I didn't need it. I had an entire, full, boundlessly fascinating life to attend to. The internet was icing on the cake. It wasn't a thing I needed, and it was barely a thing I wanted. Had Mom given us the choice between getting a modem for Christmas or a Nintendo 64, or had the choice even been between a modem and a sketchbook, I know exactly what I would have asked for. The internet was a place I went to, and it never became the destination I arrived at when running from something. I had books for that, I had anime for that, I had church for that, I had my own imagination for that. But—and here is where privilege and luck shine most brightly—there wasn't all that much around me to run away from. Aside from a death in the family near the tail end of the 1990s, there was precious little calamity. I had everything I needed.

But I think I'm cool, now, with the possibility that that has changed. The internet never has been and never will be purely a dopamine delivery service. You can order more appropriate medication than that. It's more than ambient anxiety and too much human contact. It's more than the effervescent, the fleeting, the fingertips reaching from their respective boats to touch over storm-tossed seas. It's where you can order groceries, bookshelves. If you have that oh-so-precious JSTOR access, it's where you can find help with your homework. It's WhatsApp group chats with your extended family in the Old Country. It's Zooming for work. It's Skyping for love. With all this talk of whether or not the internet is good for us, all this talk about what it's done to our hearts, to our minds, to our souls, it's easy to forget how useful it is. How necessary.

That tax, though. Determining whether passage through the Portal is for the better or for the worse is a nigh-impossible task. What's on the other side is always changing, and sometimes the effect is that of lower air quality and you come back to your life choking, your lungs scarred from all that methane; and sometimes the effect is the warm embrace of a familiar. Sometimes the effect is that tickling of the Shadow Self, and sometimes it is some anonymous stranger on the other end of a game chat unknowingly nudging you in the opposite direction. Sometimes, the effect is that of diversion, distraction, however necessary, and sometimes we enter the Portal with pure and unadorned purpose. Increasingly, these days, we wear the Portal—on our wrists, in our pockets, etc.—and an effort needs to be made to escape the ping, the notification, the Pavlovian impulse to check and see what has changed in your life since the last one. And when the Portal does start to become the very air you breathe, it becomes even more difficult to conduct a moral accounting of the changes wrought by passage through it.

I used to think the internet was like a drug, not because it was addictive, but because it tended to render the user in italics. However much you thought you had changed when you became your online self, that second person was inside your skin all along. Any exogenous shock merely chipped away at the marble to reveal the sculpture beneath. But there's simply too much of us for that to be true. What I mean is that there's too much of you—you, the individual—for that to be true.

There's no single self that the internet endeavors to uncover, no singular specter behind the mask. Because the internet is us. The internet is Legion, for we are many.

Has it really taken me an entire book to get to this point? This understanding? That the constitutional theorist and the writer of spy novels and the Black anime geek and the gamer whose favorite band is System of a Down and whose favorite essayist is Patricia Lockwood, this guy who used to write papers on transnational criminal organizations and now writes books about gentrifiers from space, you mean to tell me they're all the same guy? And that he's the same guy who streamed three *Elden Ring* playthroughs on Twitch?

Though *Sehnsucht* has no true analogue in English, it does vibe with the Portuguese *saudade*, that melancholic longing for something or someone so distant as to be ever unreachable. Incompleteness defines these two words, and often the thing that would complete us doesn't exist, or we don't know what it is, or both of those things are the case, each of us a bisected sphere from Plato's *Symposium* questing eternally for our other half.

Goethe's "Nur wer die Sehnsucht kennt" ("Only Those Who Know Longing") from his novel *Wilhelm Meister's Apprenticeship*, was set to music by Beethoven. The poem goes like this:

> Nur wer die Sehnsucht kennt
> Weiß, was ich leide!

> Allein und abgetrennt
> Von aller Freude
> Seh' ich an's Firmament
> Nach jener Seite.
> Ach, der mich liebt und kennt,
> Ist in der Weite.
> Es schwindelt mir, es brennt
> Mein Eingeweide.
> Nur wer die Sehnsucht kennt
> Weiß, was ich leide!

While I do chuckle at the thought of me shouting this poem in German to the heavens, I have spent much of this collection, much of this essay, feeling as dramatic as any rendering or performance of this poem might deserve. That longing, for an old place, for an old internet, for that workshop, for that spy novelist, for some amalgamation of those things, it's been powerful enough to squeeze fifty thousand words out of me. And yet only here at the end do I realize how Janus-faced a concept is *Sehnsucht*. All this time, I thought the key to my multiplicity, to exhibiting that multiplicity online, lay in retrieving a previous self. In reality, this manifold self is a thing I am building, a thing we are all building one tweet, one Angelfire webpage, one sentence at a time.

I don't know what a fully realized Web 3.0 will look like, whether it will be entirely dystopian, replete with stolen art made into uncopyrightable work and blockchain-this and NFT-that. Or whether it will be something else entirely, something just as promising, just as expansive, just as capable of fitting the entirety of our selves as what came before.

Perhaps it will, perhaps we will, be even more than that.

Acknowledgments

First and foremost, I must thank my agent, Noah Ballard, for nudging me so insistently into trying my hand at an essay collection. My thanks, as well, to Roxane Gay for her enthusiasm and guidance during this entire process and to Irena Huang for her diligence. Any book would be a much lesser book without the work of the intrepid copyeditors who worked on it, so my thanks to you, Alicia. My gratitude extends to everyone at Grove Atlantic who touched this labor of love.

Several of these essays were lucky enough to find homes before making their way here. "I Have a Rendezvous with Death" appeared in *Ploughshares*, and I will be forever grateful to Laila Lalami not only for her stewardship in bringing that piece to press but also, more than that, for her friendship. "Pretty Woman," "White Bears in Sugar Land," "I Have No Mouth and I Must Scream: The Duty of the Black Writer

During Times of American Unrest," and "Select Difficulty" all appeared in slightly different form on Tor.com (now Reactor), and to Christina Orlando, I must give thanks.

I am as yet an amateur of the form, so I wear my influences prominently. To those essayists and journalists whose lyrical felicity, whose insight, and whose eternal curiosity have made such an impact on me—especially, but not exclusively, Tom Bissell, Leslie Jamison, Patricia Lockwood, Jacqueline Rose, and Ta-Nehisi Coates—my utmost gratitude for opening my eyes to what truly dope things are possible with the essay.

References

Is This a Race Book?

Blake, Meredith, and Yvonne Villarreal. 2023. "In Past Strikes, Networks Turned to Reality TV. Now It's More Complicated." *Los Angeles Times*, April 10. https://www.latimes.com/entertainment-arts/business/story/2023-04-10/writers-strike-reality-tv-unions.

"Changing Media Landscape Takes Center Stage in Strike." 2007. CNN. November 8. http://www.cnn.com/2007/SHOWBIZ/TV/11/08/strike.impact/index.html.

Doctorow, Cory. 2023. "The 'Enshittification' of TikTok." *WIRED*. January 23. https://www.wired.com/story/tiktok-platforms-cory-doctorow/.

Kramer, Adam D. I., Jamie E. Guillory, and Jeffrey T. Hancock. 2014. "Experimental Evidence of Massive-Scale

Emotional Contagion through Social Networks." *Proceedings of the National Academy of Sciences* 111 (24): 8788–90. https://doi.org/10.1073/pnas.1320040111.

Meredith, Sam. 2018. "Facebook–Cambridge Analytica: A Timeline of the Data Hijacking Scandal." CNBC. April 10. https://www.cnbc.com/2018/04/10/facebook-cambridge-analytica-a-timeline-of-the-data-hijacking-scandal.html.

"Meta Reports Fourth Quarter and Full Year 2023 Results; Initiates Quarterly Dividend." 2023. Fb.com. December. https://investor.fb.com/investor-news/press-release-details/2024/Meta-Reports-Fourth-Quarter-and-Full-Year-2023-Results-Initiates-Quarterly-Dividend/default.aspx.

Sperling, Nicole. 2023. "How the Last Writers' Strike Changed Things Onscreen." *New York Times*, May 12. Business. https://www.nytimes.com/2023/05/12/business/media/last-hollywood-writers-strike.html.

Ugander, J., L. Backstrom, C. Marlow, and J. Kleinberg. 2012. "Structural Diversity in Social Contagion." *Proceedings of the National Academy of Sciences* 109 (16): 5962–66. https://doi.org/10.1073/pnas.1116502109.

"WGA Contract 2007 Proposals." 2007. Archive.org. October 17. https://web.archive.org/web/20080102204219/http://www.wga.org/subpage_member.aspx?id=2485.

Wu, Tim. 2017. *The Attention Merchants: The Epic Scramble to Get Inside Our Heads*. Vintage Books.

Prometheus, Patched: The Folly of the Metaverse

Badev, Anton, and Cy Watsky. 2023. "Interconnected DeFi: Ripple Effects from the Terra Collapse." *Finance and Economics Discussion Series*, no. 2023-044 (June): 1–39. https://doi.org/10.17016/feds.2023.044.

Browne, Ryan. 2022. "Tether Withdrawals Top $10 Billion as Regulators Raise Alarm about Stablecoins." CNBC. May 23. https://www.cnbc.com/2022/05/23/tether-usdt-stablecoin-withdrawals-top-10-billion.html.

DashieGames. 2019a. "OVER 40,000 PEOPLE PLAYED THIS LEVEL AND FAILED!! [SUPER MARIO MAKER 2] [#10]." YouTube video, 48 min., 2 sec. August 31. https://www.youtube.com/watch?v=o5j7xaep5XQ&list=PL1LBVGIz9_PWVXGExW1qszK11U6S9RDnA&index=34.

———. 2019b. "THIS IS THE CRUELEST LEVEL EVER MADE!! [SUPER MARIO MAKER 2] [#24]." YouTube video, 44 min., 32 sec. December 7. https://www.youtube.com/watch?v=y9eyg2S3hE4&list=PL1LBVGIz9_PWVXGExW1qszK11U6S9RDnA&index=35.

———. 2020. "BRO.. HOW IS THIS EVEN POSSIBLE!? HOW!? [SUPER MARIO MAKER 2] [#59]." YouTube. August 8. https://www.youtube.com/watch?v=AyLi-7YXbSU&list=PL1LBVGIz9_PWVXGExW1qszK11U6S9RDnA&index=37.

———. 2021. "MUST WATCH! INCREDIBLY HARD LEVELS!! [SUPER MARIO MAKER 2] [#97]." YouTube video, 42 min. August 18. https://www.youtube.com/watch?v=gebtDQA_Hmw&list=PL1LBVGIz9_PWVXGExW1qszK11U6S9RDnA&index=35.

Hern, Alex. 2022. "Tether Pays Out $10bn in Withdrawals since Start of Crypto Crash." *Guardian*. May 22. https://www.theguardian.com/technology/2022/may/22/tether-pays-out-10bn-in-withdrawal-since-crypto-crash.

Leswing, Kif. 2022. "Meta Lost $2.8 Billion on Its Virtual Reality Ambitions During Q2." CNBC. July 27. https://www.cnbc.com/2022/07/27/meta-reality-labs-lost-2point8-billion-in-q2-2022.html.

Levy, Ari, and MacKenzie Sigalos. 2022. "Crypto Peaked a Year Ago—Investors Have Lost More Than $2 Trillion Since." CNBC. November 11. https://www.cnbc.com/2022/11/11/crypto-peaked-in-nov-2021-investors-lost-more-than-2-trillion-since.html.

Miller, Rosemarie. 2023. "Meta Takes 2.8 Billion Dollar Loss on Its Metaverse Bet." *Forbes*, October 4. https://www.forbes.com/sites/rosemariemiller/2022/07/28/meta-takes-28-billion-dollar-loss-on-its-metaverse-bet/.

Quiroz-Gutierrez, Marco. 2023. "Meta's Reality Labs Lost $13.7 Billion in 2022—and Just Reported Its Worst Quarter Ever." *Fortune*. February 1. https://fortune.com/crypto/2023/02/01/after-losing-13-billion-in-2022-metas-reality-labs-just-had-its-worst-quarter-ever/.

Vanian, Jonathan, and Ari Levy. 2023. "Meta Lost $13.7 Billion on Reality Labs in 2022 as Zuckerberg's Metaverse

Bet Gets Pricier." CNBC. February 1. https://www.cnbc.com/2023/02/01/meta-lost-13point7-billion-on-reality-labs-in-2022-after-metaverse-pivot.html.

Varanasi, Lakshmi. 2023. "Mark Zuckerberg's Metaverse Just Keeps Losing Money, as Meta's Reality Labs Division Posts a Loss of $13.7 Billion for the Year." *Business Insider*. February 1. https://www.businessinsider.com/meta-reality-labs-metaverse-lost-1b-more-than-year-ago-2023-2.

Yaffe-Bellany, David, Erin Griffith, and Ephrat Livni. 2022. "Cryptocurrencies Melt Down in a 'Perfect Storm' of Fear and Panic." *New York Times*, May 12. Technology. https://www.nytimes.com/2022/05/12/technology/cryptocurrencies-crash-bitcoin.html.

Zuckerberg, Mark. 2021a. "Facebook, Inc. (FB) Third Quarter 2021 Results Conference Call." October 25. https://s21.q4cdn.com/399680738/files/doc_financials/2021/q3/FB-Q3-2021-Earnings-Call-Transcript.pdf.

———. 2021b. "Founder's Letter, 2021." Meta. October 28. https://about.fb.com/news/2021/10/founders-letter/.

Pretty Woman

Doane, Mary Ann. 2000. "Technophilia: Technology, Representation, and the Feminine." In *The Gendered Cyborg: A Reader*, edited by Gill Kirkup et al. Routledge.

Villiers de l'Isle-Adam, Auguste. (1926) 1928. *The Future Eve*. Translated by Florence Crew-Jones. Argosy.

In the original French:

> Il lui prit la main: c'était la main d'Alicia! Il respira le cou, le sein oppressé de la vision: c'était bien Alicia! Il regarda les yeux ... c'étaient bien les yeux ... seulement le regard était sublime! La toilette, l'allure ... –et ce mouchoir dont elle essuyait, en silence, deux larmes sur ses joues liliales,–c'était bien elle encore ... mais transfigurée! devenue enfin, digne de sa beauté même: l'identité idéalisée.

White Bears in Sugar Land

Bould, Mark. 2007. "The Ships Landed Long Ago: Afrofuturism and Black SF." *Science Fiction Studies* 34 (2): 177–86.

Okoye, Florence. 2016. "There Are Black People in the Future." *How We Get to Next*. January 7. https://www.howwegettonext.com/there-are-black-people-in-the-future/.

I Have No Mouth and I Must Scream: The Duty of the Black Writer During Times of American Unrest

Demby, Gene. 2015. "How Black Reporters Report on Black Death." NPR.org. August 20. https://www.npr.org/sections/codeswitch/2015/08/20/432590298/how-black-reporters-report-on-black-death.

Select Difficulty

Bissell, Tom. 2010. *Extra Lives*. Vintage Books.

Deus in Machina

James 4:3 (KJV).

Complicated German Words Regarding Memory

1 Corinthians 13:11.
Beethoven, Ludwig van. "Sehnsucht," WoO 134.
Bell Jr., Derrick. 1978. "The Racial Imperative in American Law." In *The Age of Segregation: Race Relations in the South, 1890–1945*, 3–28. University Press of Mississippi.

Ely, John Hart. 1980. *Democracy and Distrust*. Harvard University Press.

Goethe, Johann Wolfgang von. 1795. *Wilhelm Meisters Lehrjahre*. Johann Friedrich Unger (Berlin).

Lehane, Dennis. 2008. *The Given Day*. William Morrow.

Roberts, Dorothy E. 1997. "The Meaning of Blacks' Fidelity to the Constitution." *Fordham Law Review* 65 (4): 1761.

Wright, Richard. 1940. *Native Son*. Vintage Books